A journey from NOWHERE TO NOWHERE!

Based on a true story

Manzitha Sokupa

A Journey from Nowhere to Nowhere

Published by Manzitha Sokupa

Contact Details ManzithaPen@gmail.com

ISBN 978-0-620-80624-4

eISBN 978-0-620-80625-1

2 4 6 8 10 9 7 5 3 1

Cover by Manzitha Sokupa

Layout and publication facilitation by Boutique Books

Printed in South Africa by Digital Action

Acknowledgements

FIRST OF ALL, I THANK the Almighty, my Creator, for the gift of life, good health, family, friends, *love* and all my abilities. I would not have been able to start and finish this project without Your grace.

I thank AmaSango amahle, ooNzitha, Nyandemnyam'eng-athwalwa ngabafazi, Phantsolo, Khwayikhwayi, Mlungwan'omnyama noThsanana, Manyathela ngentsimbi, Mgabhisa, Ngxwangxwa. Aaa! Sango! Nabo ooNyawuza, ooThahla kandayeni, ooHlamba ngobende amanzi ekhona, ooZiqelekazi, ooFaku, ooNgqungqushe, ooSiphunzi somthathi somthole siqutywa singeva, Aa! Ngcwangula! Tita! for guidance and clarity when sometimes I feel confused.

I thank my family for allowing me the space to write this piece, for understanding my cause and for supporting me throughout with facts where I was not so sure anymore. I would not have been able to finish this book without you.

My parents and my four siblings, I thank you for your love but most of all I thank you for understanding. To my two children, Simanye and Okuhle, thank you for your support – for the reminders and encouragement, especially the times when I didn't feel like going on. You understood how important writing this book was for my well-being. The ideas and opinions around the book cover are appreciated. You are awesome and I love you.

To my best friend Mide, thank you for making me finally put it down on paper, for being the first to read it when it was still very raw, for your invaluable contribution and guidance. You also understood the importance of this book to my well-being and everyone involved.

I can't overemphasise the extent of everyone's support throughout this two-year-long project. I am honoured and humbled.

From my heart, *Enkosi! ndiyabulela!*

⚬⚬⚬⚬⚬ **Prologue** ⚬⚬⚬⚬⚬

EVERYBODY GOES THROUGH HARD TIMES, but there is nothing that can justify this cruel act! Shh! Don't judge! It's easy to say whatever you like when you are not on the receiving end, without knowing what really went down. Why are you even trying to rationalise this? Everybody has a decision to make at the end of the day – to whose advantage doesn't matter at times. One's got to do what one's got to do!

I've always felt strongly about protecting my loved ones and sometimes even get biased, or perhaps more often than not. But one thing that really upsets me is seeing kids hurt… even way before I had my own. It just would literally stop my heartbeat and I guess it has got worse now that I have mine. The thought of them being lost somewhere or stranded, wondering where I am, just cripples me.

Hold on my dear! I touch my chest and literally feel my heart racing. Anxious as I am, I manage to sit down on the staircase at my workplace, looking around to see if anyone is looking. What's most upsetting about some bad decisions that are taken for children, or about children, is that they are mostly about the decision maker; how *they* feel, how *they* are not able to do this or that. Sometimes I think it's almost as if people think that children don't have feelings. *"Maybe you are just being a child yourself that's why you feel like this, young lady. You know nothing about being in the shoes of a parent.*" Mhmm! Somebody once said that having children or giving birth to a child doesn't make one a parent; it takes more than that, maybe that's what I still need to find out and maybe then I'll understand.

This conversation continued in my head for a while. 'What would happen if I didn't have my own children? Would I feel different, maybe? What on earth would make me leave my children behind and never look back? Poverty maybe…? Huh! Or struggling due to lack of employment, maybe? Well, I'm not convinced.

"Maybe you should try and be in their shoes just for once!" is what people will say. "Try not to judge. Maybe they are better than those who kill their children. Instead, they leave them for other people to find and raise when they themselves could not.'

Those words have become common in our society. Over and over again, people find themselves having to understand the evil that other people do on a daily basis. Nothing can make me understand the hardships that a mother must have been through to abandon her children and to never look back, weighing it against how the children will be impacted by the decision and how the ones who discover these children must feel at that very first moment of finding them. Maybe they are better off; maybe they are not. Maybe I don't know better…

I don't really know to whose advantage this decision is, but I, being a mother, believe that I would never leave my children. I would never abandon my children... this can never be to their advantage. Agh! When mothers decide to abandon their children, people have to stop a bit and try to be in their shoes to try to understand, just for once. Why can't the same principle be applied to the other side of the equation? Why can't people stop a bit for once, and try to put themselves in these children's shoes? For me, this principle should be applied to both sides or not at all. One would see the impact this has on both sides. After all, people react differently to situations and some demons seem to be better than others… it seems our society has learned to accept things and is able to measure which devils are better than others.

I've seen some children, mostly babies and toddlers, who have been tied up on the bed inside a shack and locked there by their mothers and left there to die. Had it not been for that angel who came to their rescue, they would have eventually died. Some of these babies end up with a deformity as a result of lying on the floor on one side of their face for weeks. In other instances, they get choked and thrown down toilet pits. I guess that this is where we find ourselves as a society on almost a daily basis; hence all these measurements of how evil one action is when measured against other horrific actions.

I won't lie to myself: I'm angry with this woman called Jackie, and I won't convince myself that I am not. I'm angry for my siblings, for their unimaginable pain and the answers that my entire family could not give them; the answers that I too could not give them. Not unless I could find her and bring her to come and speak for herself. The words "we love you" alone didn't carry much weight anymore. Even I felt the emptiness of my words every time I spoke them. Even though I knew I meant them, it was not important as the people they were intended for found them difficult to believe.

A Journey from Nowhere to Nowhere

1992

IN A BEAUTIFUL VILLAGE CALLED Ngcele, on the soil of Jamangile back in the Eastern Cape, is where I grew up as a little girl. My home is situated at the top of the village and, due to its exposure to the strong winds, my father had planted trees to surround the whole front part of the yard from one side to the other. He would trim these trees so beautifully to make them well shaped. The same trees would give nice shade when the sun was intense.

My parent's house was four-roomed: two bedrooms, and an open plan kind of arrangement with a sitting room combined with dining room and kitchen. It had a veranda and there were three entrances to it: one leading straight to the kitchen, one to the second room and the other to the sitting room. If people were sitting in the kitchen, someone sitting in the lounge would still be able to see them and be able to have a conversation with them.

A few metres from this house was my granny's house and a rondavel. We were a poor family – didn't have much – but there was a warmth that just drew people from all over the place to come and stay there. My parents had a total of five children of their own, including me, but there would always be one or two extra children – cousins and strangers – boarding and attending a local high school.

⸰⸰⸰⸰⸰ Chapter 1 ⸰⸰⸰⸰⸰

Day 1

IT WAS AFTER SCHOOL HOURS one sunny afternoon. The schools were out and children were going to their homes. Playing touch, running, dodging and screaming was the order of the day. Some played *upuca* or sang and played hand clapping games; we used to call that game *byshoza*. This is a game that can be played by two or more participants, with a funny song or rhyme going with it. Some were playing "my in" or playing skipping rope games. We used to call skipping rope *ugqaphu*. Both boys and girls of my age, then, could play all the games. It's just hilarious to actually realise that what was supposed to be "am I in?" had become "my in!" What is even funnier is that even a lot of kids of today still call this game "my in".

Who even knows what the real name of the game we used to call *byshoza* is? In fact, I asked my children and nephews to play *byshoza* because I wanted to hear if the lyrics would make sense, because back then we sang almost anything, adding our own words that didn't always make sense – and believe me, most of the time we didn't understand them. Surely you can't blame us for not knowing English and naming certain things in the vernacular. As I listened to them play the game, I couldn't help but laugh. Nothing has changed. These kids still sing exactly the same way we did. I can't argue with them because they are much more clued up than we were then. Anyway, "my in" also required that a certain pattern be drawn on the floor with numbers ranging from one to eight, if I remember correctly, but then a player would need to close their eyes or look up so as not to see the pattern and attempt to enter all those boxes in the pattern, asking the other participants on the outside if he or she is in.

As much as we'd be hungry and wanting to get home as soon as possible so we could eat, it was not possible to escape all the fun games. My favourite game was *upuca,* but I also loved playing touch because I was a master of running and dodging. I loved playing *upuca* because I could focus and I was fast in terms of the hand and eye coordination that was required by the game – which required throwing one stone up and getting the rest out of the circle and catching the stone that you threw up and taking those that you took out of the circle back to the circle and leaving only one outside the circle until all the stones that were in the circle have been taken out of that circle.

In all these fun games, falling and getting bruised was inevitable. From time to time, I would get home with either a bleeding knee or one of my toes cut open from tripping. Also, in between, there'd be a bit of fighting because tempers got lost in the middle of the games. *Upuca* was a bit of a time waster because we would need to sit down in order to play it, but I loved it nonetheless. This would irritate the learners who were older than us and those who came from the local high schools, as we would literally sit in the middle of the road – for obvious reasons, of course. One, you can't draw the circle in the grass and two you can't play with small stones in the grass. Remember that this type of grass is not the kind that you find in front of these nice yards we see in town; not lawn. I'm talking about the long grass that would be up to my waist at that time. The chances of losing school clothing items and books in all that were also very high.

What is funny now is that I never used to understand why it was such a big deal to Mom if I lost a shoe or jersey in that process. As a kid, it's very easy to lose clothing items and unfortunately you don't have a clue how they got lost. The only thing that is on your mind when the bell rings is to grab your plastic bag with your books, and your jersey will either be tied around your waist or put on your shoulder with one arm hanging loose while everybody competes to get to the school gate. If that jersey falls off in the process of running, you won't feel it. Plus, with all the buzz, if your plastic bag has a hole in it and one of your shoes falls out you won't notice – not unless someone who really cares sees it and alerts you to it, but there are very few chances of that. In fact, most if not all the time I'd only find out that I had only one shoe the following morning, when I wanted to put them on for school.

My younger sister and I, together with some children from my village would get home eventually, covered with dust, looking as if we hadn't had a bath or even seen water for a number of days, let alone since the morning before going to school. It would get even worse if particular attention was paid to just above the mouth area. Sunny or cold, some would have a running tap over there, and others would have dry white lines, like the dusty paths in the village. I remember our teachers would shout at you for either having a *umlungu* peeping out from your nose or for having that dusty path that was an indication that the *umlungu* they were talking about had not just peeped out from the nose but had actually exited and left a mark there. Sometimes I still wonder why the mucus was called an *umlungu* and still is. I often hear my nephews tease one another about having one peeping out from the nose, even now.

The parents and other adults who were fortunate and had jobs would still be at work and some who were not working would have gone either to the river to do their washing or would be busy in their gardens. You would find both women and young men, especially the high school boarders who attended a local high school in my village at the river, washing their blankets, school uniform or queuing to get water. Jamangile High School was popular because it produced quality matric results and attracted multitudes of learners from the neighbouring towns and villages. Many of them boarded in our homes for a monthly rental of twenty to thirty Rand per learner per month. In summer, some people would spread their blankets and mats on the grass or on those huge rocks that grace the river bank in order to dry them before they took them home.

Fortunately, my home was in very close proximity to the river; hence carrying the wet washing wasn't as much of an issue as it was for some other villagers. The problem with this idea of spreading the mats and blankets on the grass or rocks by the river bank was that sometimes there were cows that would not be driven to the veld by their owners and they would harass the people and eat the washing. Once a clothing item has been chewed by a cow, one can never get it right again, so these people had to actually be on the lookout for the cows, even if they had to leave the items and go home to do other chores while things dried.

I had just turned seven years old. Out of five siblings I was the fourth child and also the first girl after three boys, followed by my sister, the last born. My sister was yet to turn five later in the year. We attended the same school, where I was busy with Standard 1 and she was in Sub A. We would walk together to school in the mornings, joining many other children who were also going to the same school as us and others who were going to the other schools.

Ngcele is a big location with quite a number of schools. In my village there was a high school called Jamangile S. S. S, and then you had Ntywenka with Mabandla J. S. S and Magwaxaza J. P. S, Mtshezi with Ntaba J. S. S, eDown with Ngcele J. S. S, my school, Ngxaza J. S. S and Thandisizwe High school at Mountain. This number of schools alone should indicate the amount of the traffic to school on a normal day. Going to school in the morning was always a mission. We would always be late because, one, the school was far away and I think that any seven-year-old or any five-year-old can only do so much in terms of walking fast. And, two, the legs are just too short – and of course playing would also play a big part on the delay.

Sometimes the mornings would just be marred by tears. Either I don't want to go to school because I didn't have a pencil, or I had lost my book and I was afraid of that certain horrible teacher, or I wanted twenty cents to carry to school so my sister and I could buy two spoons of Morvite that was sold at a spaza shop beside the school, and my mother didn't have the money. So many reasons, and sometimes we would even end up getting a hiding for toyi-toying in the mornings.

On this particular day, my younger sister and I were coming home from school along with other learners – tired, hungry and with a distance of twelve kilometres to walk back home. It took us almost two hours and sometimes even more to get home from school every day, as we were playing with other kids and taking rests along the way. We got home, looking forward to finding out if there was something to eat, to taking off our school uniforms, to looking for our granny and then going off to play. As usual, there was no one at my mother's house. The house was closed and locked, but we knew the spot where we'd find keys on the veranda just as we did every day. But today, when we got home, there was something a bit unusual.

"There are people sitting under the trees," my sister alerted me just as we approached the gate. When I looked up, as we came closer towards the house, I realised that indeed there were people sitting in the shade under the trees. That was not my problem and probably not hers either. We grew up in a home where there were always people coming there, but sitting on a mattress with suitcases outside of the house was a bit odd. We had never seen anything like it before. What made things even worse was that these were not just people; there was an *umlungu* girl with them.

People would come to our home and would stay for some time, either attending a nearby high school or for some or other reason, but we were just kids, too young to be worried about the details of why a specific somebody was staying at our home with us. The other thing was that most people would arrive and find us with our parents at home. We had never experienced finding anybody waiting for us at home, let alone with a mattress and a suitcase and a white child on top of that. We just saw these two women with two children; one child wore a red top with a hoodie and a red skirt and gumboots on her feet, while the second child, still a small baby, wore a waterproof at the bottom and a t-shirt with red and white stripes on top.

The girl looked extremely light in complexion, with long blonde and curly hair. I was convinced I was seeing an *umlungu,* as we would call her in my language. We were startled, I must say. Now, for the first moment this was a bit weird and I got a little scared.

"*Umlungu!*" my sister burst out before I could say anything. I quickly pulled her closer to me and we marched towards the house.

"Shhh!" I cautioned. "Are you not afraid of these people?" I asked.

"Maybe they are going to steal us," she said, whispering this time. Her eyes were wide open and her brows were furrowed.

"I also don't know, *mos!*" I shrugged my shoulders. "Maybe they are giants and they want to steal children and eat them?"

     A Journey from Nowhere to Nowhere

A second question followed from my concerned sister. "Mhm! Could they be giants?"

I felt this unsettling sensation in my stomach, now that Zitha was planting a seed of fear in my mind. "No man, those bedtime stories that our granny used to tell us had never featured a giant that had children. Most giants never had children and maybe that's why they always ate other people's children," I thought.

"No! shhh! Remember, Granny said that giants are huge – maybe as big as our house or a big tree? These people are not giants. Now let's go."

There had been a sense of anxiety in my sister's voice and I must say she was slowly exerting fear in me as well. If she didn't stop with her crazy questions, I was on the verge of just throwing that plastic bag with my books down and running for my life to my granny's house. Why I had not done this in the first place is that I did not see any danger in there being people at my home, but was just shocked to see *umlungu* at my home. We'd never seen a white person that close in our lives. I'm not a very dark person either in complexion, but this little girl stood out. She had this long blonde hair, big blue eyes; very tiny, very light in weight, and she had a big nose, even though it was not sharp. It was difficult to estimate the girl's age at that moment, but she looked smaller and tinier than my soon-to-be-five sister.

The other child was a baby, still crawling, but he looked more like the people we were used to in terms of his complexion. He was crawling in the space in front of the mattress, picking up things from the ground and bringing them to his mouth. I could hear one of the women calling him and trying to lure him back to the mattress, but this baby was just doing his own thing. They did not seem bothered by our arrival. The one who looked older was smoking a cigarette and chatting together with the second woman. They looked normal, much like us, even though the one with a cigarette was a bit darker and the other was a bit of a yellow bone.

"*Molweni*, aunty!" we greeted in our mother tongue, with my sister just doing the last part of the greeting. We passed quickly, with my arm around my sister's shoulders as some form of protection, I guess. I don't remember if they greeted us back because I was mostly interested in getting past them as soon as possible. Just as soon as we got to the veranda I put down my "No problem" plastic bag with my books and looked for the key in the usual spot.

"Open quickly, I'm starving," said my sister.

"Okay, hold on! I'm trying here," I responded. I pulled over an empty five litre bucket of paint to climb on so I could reach the lock. Phew! Finally! I grinned when the door at last opened. As soon as we entered, I pulled a chair closer to the table and climbed up to get some water for us to drink from a bucket on top of the table. "Have some, I know you are thirsty." I handed over a not-so-white jug to her. I opened each pot that was on the table and on top of the flame stove looking for something for us to eat. "Mhm! seems like there's no food besides this." I showed her the pot that had samp and beans. There was a funny smell but…

"Come on, let's eat!" she interjected before I could even finish talking. I took the pot and went outside the house and placed the pot on the floor of the veranda. I asked her to keep an eye on the food as I quickly went back inside to get spoons. I knew that Box, our dog, wouldn't waste time helping herself to our food if we left it there unmanned. Already she was there in anticipation; as if we were making food for her. Maybe she was hungry also; maybe it had been a long day for her as well. For the moment, we were so preoccupied by the food and the hunger that we forgot about our strange guests outside.

Just as we sat on our heels, ready to dig from the pot, the *umlungu* girl approached. "Eyi, she's coming," my sister whispered. I looked on as she got closer and closer. She squatted at the pot, just like we did, focusing on what was in the pot. There was a bit of silence for a moment, as we watched her very carefully.

"*Uyafuna ukutya?*" I asked her. She just looked at me as if she were blank and there was no response. Remember, in those days I knew nothing about English, let alone being able to speak it. I mean, really, I was just seven. I still had a lot to figure out, even in my own mother language, *Isixhosa*. All we knew as kids at that time was that aeroplanes brought our parents babies and we believed that we could also get some gifts from those aeroplanes. Somehow we understood that one had to speak English to them in order to be heard, and as a result we used to shout at every aeroplane flying up in the sky and our attempt to speak English would be "*Vityo! Vityo! Umngqusho uvuthiwe.*" You can ask me some other time who came up with that line and how they came up with it and what it meant.

I didn't know what to say to her and I decided to ignore her. We continued to eat and I watched her as we ate. She would look at the pot and follow our hands all the way to our mouths, again and again. "Okay, I think she's hungry just like us," I said. My sister gave me a look, with a mouthful of stamp and beans, and simply shrugged her shoulders as a sign of "I don't know". I stood up to get a spoon for her from inside the house and I handed it to her. By this time the baby was also crawling towards where we were sitting. I guessed one had to try to make signs; maybe the girl would get what I was trying to get across to her.

After giving her the spoon, I looked at her and I looked at the pot and pointed to it with my head. From there, I was ready to give up but, guess what? Mhh! she got it. She started to eat, even though she hesitated for a few moments. My sister and I stopped and watched her eat. After a brief moment of silence, I resorted to the sign language to my sister, now pointing with my head for her to eat. I could see the facial expressions on both of them: the food was a bit off. It tasted awful to me, but it was either that or nothing. The food had probably spoilt due to the heat.

The crawling baby had finally made it to the veranda; his hands were covered with sand and he was drooling. I looked at my spoon and I looked at my sister. I have always loved babies; they are just so cute. I couldn't help myself. Even though he was dirty, I wondered if I could pick him up just once, but I was afraid of the two women.

"Are you going to give him?" my sister asked. All the while the baby was trying to get to the pot.

"Never! When his mouth is like that?" I responded and quickly grabbed the pot and stood up. This guy meant business, his hand was reaching for the pot and he was going to put sand in our food. My sister stood up also, looking almost as if she were running away from the baby. We just laughed at him sitting there alone. I handed the pot to my sister but she didn't want to take it.

"I'm full also, *mos*, give it to her," she said, moving backwards into the house. I dug into the pot and fed the baby. Nha! He didn't like it. He just spat it all out and started blowing bubbles with lots of saliva.

"Sies!" I looked at my spoon and it was just a mixture of soil, saliva and the food; that was disgusting. I rubbed my spoon on my dress. Shaking my head, I went inside the house.

Zitha just laughed at me and said, "I told you, Zowi. Look at your spoon now". His neck and chest were actually wet and, now that I think of it, it must have been the saliva that made him wet. Anyway, after we had finished eating we tried getting rid of the girl by making sounds and making hand gestures so that she would go back to the aunties under the trees, but it didn't work.

I had an idea. "Let's run fast and leave her," I whispered in my sister's ear.

"Okay." She nodded her head in agreement and we sped off towards my granny's house, leaving my mother's house door wide open as the girl was inside the house with us. That didn't seem to work well as she also started running after us.

"Iyoo, she's catching up," we laughed as we ran past the rondavel. "Granny! Granny!" we called out as we approached the stairs of her house – but no response.

"Maybe she is in the garden!" my sister reckoned. Indeed, she was there, working in her vegetable garden.

My grandmother was one beautiful lady; same complexion as mine. Even though she was maybe in her seventies, she was still very beautiful and strong. She had a wonderful vegetable garden where she had different kinds of vegetables: the likes of spinach, cabbage, carrots, beetroot, tomatoes, green onion, peas (but we used to call them *ertjies*) and potatoes. She used to tell me about different kinds of cabbage. We would fetch water from the river for her and put it in the gallons that were kept inside the garden, but close enough to the fence so that we didn't struggle when we ferried the water, so that she could irrigate her vegetable garden. Sometimes we helped her with the watering. If I still remember correctly, she would even sell the potatoes to other villagers who wanted to buy. In front of her house were different kinds of flowers in bright colours which attracted beautiful and colourful butterflies.

When we got to her, there was a third person with us; an *umlungu* girl who had very long hair and blue eyes. I think Granny just heard the sound of us running and giggling towards her and she didn't pay much attention. The gate to the garden was a bit tricky to open, but we didn't need it to open wide; a tiny opening was okay for us. We squeezed ourselves in there. Gasping for air, we greeted "*Makhulu*, what are you doing today?"

"*Molweni bantwana*! You guys are back finally," she responded, without looking up to see us. She was busy trying to fix the opening in the fence that had been made by pigs or goats; I can't remember correctly. As soon as she lifted her eyes, there we were. Her face changed. "*Haibo nina bantwana ndini*! Who's that you are with? Whose child is that?" There was no response. I just shrugged my shoulders. My sister is not much of a talker, so she was just sitting and playing with the soil. "*Nimfumana phi umlungu nina bantwana ndini?*" she exclaimed in her big but soft voice. We were concerned now because we had not brought this child along; she had followed us.

"We didn't get her, *Makhulu*," we responded in a chorus, with my sister finishing after me. Actually, she liked saying what I was saying, now that I think about it. My eyes are big naturally but they were now even bigger. I shrugged my shoulders and looked at Granny. I anticipated that she was going to shout at us. I mean, we hadn't brought the girl. We'd tried to chase her to her people but she'd kept on following us; hence we'd come running.

Granny was still looking for an answer that I didn't have. "*Nkosi enofefe! Ngumhlola ke ngoku lo! Baphambene na ababantwana Thixo?*"

"We don't know, *Makhulu*," I said.

"We found her there and it's Zowi who said we must run and leave her there," my sister explained, this time pointing in the direction of my mother's house and blaming me in the middle of it.

"Where?" Granny asked. She seemed genuinely concerned by this.

"There are people seated under the shade inside the yard by our mom's house," we tried to explain to her.

"Don't talk nonsense here, you two! Where are you getting this child from?" she asked again, now with a stern voice and a look of disbelief. She clapped her hands and looked down at what she was doing for a moment *"Ingaba ngobani abobantu? Khona! Bafunantoni apha? Nomlungu nakhona? Yho!"* she clapped again. At that moment we were not answering her anymore because she was talking to herself. Instead, we started playing with the soil in the garden and from there we went to play with our self-made toys. She stood there for a few minutes, probably trying to process what we just told her and what she was seeing and she continued with what she was doing. I think at that time she must have realised that we were only kids and would sincerely not have answers for her.

She must have gone out of the garden to go and have a look. My mother had been working at one of the homes in the village as a domestic worker, or "the help", as it is referred to nowadays. She took care of the house and children in that house while their parents were away at work. She would leave in the morning and come back in the afternoon. Her place of work was not far away from my home but was in the lower part of the village and, because of the trees in front of our house and the landscape, she would not have been able to see any movements at home from where she was, although one could see the front of the houses where she worked from our place. So, I want to think that my granny must have called her from there because it was not long after that that my mother came back, even though it was a bit earlier than usual.

We got to our play houses and started playing but this girl was still following us. My sister and I started talking about her and her long hair that almost reached her lower back; it was the first time that we had seen a person with such long hair and she looked like a doll. As much as my mother used to primp our hair, it never grew that long before it started breaking and was cut by Granny again and again. When this girl sat down, I passed an empty bottle of cooking oil to her – that would be her doll going forward until she could find another one that she liked. Remember that we didn't have dolls and we used to make our dolls with empty bottles and, depending on the size of the bottle, we'd make families; from kids to moms and dads.

The play didn't get anywhere as I noticed that my sister was just staring at this girl and admiring her hair. We started touching her hair. It was soft and curly, as well as rich and puffy. Sitting still, she didn't complain but watched us as if she didn't understand what we were doing and at the same time she could not express herself. Our play houses were anywhere we decided to sit and play; be it at the stairs of the veranda or just beside the house. We were not allowed to bring our dirty bottles inside the house. We'd have to play with our shoes and make them babies if we played inside the house. I remember one of the two women calling out and the girl stood up and went towards the house from where the voice came. After a while she came back with her hair nicely tied with a pom-pom at the back.

"Wow! Look at that," my sister exclaimed. "They've tied the hair. Maybe it's because it is too long, nhe?" she asked me and I just nodded my head in agreement. Meanwhile, the girl came back and sat down where she had been seated before and she took her "doll". My sister still continued to touch her hair. She gave the girl her doll in exchange for playing with her hair.

Now that I'm older and think about it, maybe if we'd had a TV at home back then, our reactions would have been different. We would have seen people like her in terms of the colour as well as people with such long hair, and maybe if we'd had proper dolls we would have seen and experienced touching such long hair, even if it were not real. I can't help thinking about what our reaction would have been if things had not occurred in the nineties but in the year 2000 instead.

I mean, with all these colour televisions and smart phones, it's easy to see pictures of things the way they are.

It was not long after that everybody, including my mother, started to arrive. When my mother came, we ran to her as usual, and this girl followed us, even though she couldn't keep up with our speed. She didn't give up until she reached us. When we reached our mother, we were out of breath, but we just wanted to report on this girl who had been following us everywhere we went. We gasped for air and started complaining to Mama about the strange girl who had been following us since we'd come back from school.

Her reaction was no different from Granny's. "*Hayi man nina*! What are you saying now? *Umlungu*! Where?" Who are these people, na?" She posed all those questions in succession and we just shrugged our shoulders as she held our hands and led us towards the gate. She greeted the women and invited them inside. With their two big suitcases and the baby, they proceeded to the house. One aunt also visited us on that day and I am convinced she must have arrived during that time we were playing house and were busy with the little girl's hair, and we never noticed her. Granny and the aunt also made their way to my mother's house.

∘∘∘∘∘ **Chapter 2** ∘∘∘∘∘

FROM WHAT **I** COULD GATHER from the conversation between the women and my mother, granny and aunt, one of the women was known to my mother.

One woman was a black South African and my family had met her a number of years back, when she had come to visit her brother who was staying at home with us back then. That's when they had seen her for the first time and they had not seen her for a number of years after that. I must have been a small baby when her brother stayed at my place, but the name was familiar to me when it kept on coming up in the conversations, with my family asking about Zwelibanzi's whereabouts. His story with my family was also one of those that you don't get to hear about often; how he ended up at my home in the first place. My grandmother did not know her as she had not relocated to Ngcele when this woman came to my home for the first time.

Her name was Thembisa. She was sister to Zwelibanzi. They were from a place called Reni in another part of the Eastern Cape, near Libode, but they had grown up living in Gauteng for most of their childhood years and maybe as a teenager for Thembisa. The other woman was a coloured and my family didn't know her, but she was introduced by Thembisa as Jackie, her friend. These two kids belonged to Jackie and the baby boy was still breastfeeding.

Mother: "Yho! Thembisa, it's been a while! How have you been? Where is your brother? And how's your brother? What directed you here after such a long time? Agh! Forgive me for throwing a lot of questions at you. I'm just surprised. I didn't expect you."

Thembisa: "Hey aunty! We are alright. My brother is in Gauteng. We are just grateful that we are still alive but life has been difficult. I lost my job and I have been jobless for a while now; so it has not been easy, aunty".

Mother: "Yho! And now where are you heading to? And who is this lady you are with?"

Thembisa: "Jackie is my friend, aunty. We have been staying together. After she lost her job I took her in as she had no place to stay with her kids and her boyfriend had dumped her. Now, when I lost my job also, it became more difficult and I also lost my own place to stay as I could not afford to pay rent anymore.

"I decided that I wanted to come back to Umtata to look for a job and she said she's coming with me. So, to answer your question, we are headed to Umtata, aunty. One of my uncles used to own a supermarket in Umtata and I'm hoping that he could give me a job. I thought I should pass here just to check on you since I have not seen you after what you did for my brother; you practically treated my brother as your own and for that we will forever be grateful."

Mother: "Okay! I see. It is really good to see you again, Thembi. We are grateful also that you thought of us when you are back home."

My father, who was also at work, joined us later in the evening and was also happy to see Thembisa again. My father worked as a builder, building beautiful homes for the people all over the Eastern Cape. Sometimes he would go to work as far off as Flagstaff, Mqanduli, Mount Fletcher, Port St Johns… but at the time he was working locally.

When he saw Thembisa, he was delighted. "Where is Zwelibanzi?" my father asked.

"He is still in Johannesburg, uncle," Thembisa answered.

All the while we were playing and our newly found friend was following us all over the place, without saying anything.

Night came and everybody had supper that my mom had prepared and sleeping arrangements were made for our visitors and we prayed and everybody went to sleep. It is worthwhile noting that when I grew up, each and every night before everybody went to bed it was a known custom to sit around the table or gather around my granny's bed – depending on where we were going to sleep; either at my mom's house or my gran's house – but it was a norm to gather together and sing a song and then pray. If my father was around, he loved to sing and he would pray and say the grace after that, but when he was not around, Mom would do the praying.

DAY 2

In the morning, it was business as usual for us going to school, leaving everyone else still in bed. My mother was working in the neighbourhood so she prepared and went to work. Another day went by and when we came back from school there were people at home, including these visitors still there, just sitting and chatting with my mother; it would seem she had come back from work early. This older coloured woman would stand up to go and light a cigarette outside every once in a while.

It was normal for us at home that a chicken would be slaughtered when there were visitors, and as a result there was meat being cooked that day.

When we came back from school, the girl was inside the house as well, playing with her younger brother. As soon as she noticed we were back, she joined us and we moved into the yard to play our *poppie huis,* as we used to call it. I remember at some stage we became uncomfortable and almost irritated by her company simply because we couldn't understand what she was saying and she also couldn't understand our language. I must admit though that one other reason, and most probably the major one, was that we were getting irritated by her presence because we felt she was crowding our space. We were so used to being just the two girls at home, and if we were not with friends at school then we played alone at home. Now, all of a sudden, there was this girl who followed us everywhere and with whom we were struggling to talk. Even if we told her to go back inside by making hand gestures so she could see that we didn't want to play with her, she just kept coming back. She probably didn't understand a word we were saying or even those hand gestures. It was either that, or she was just stubborn. Anyway, we complained to Mama. We didn't want to play with her and we were tired of being followed by her and I wanted my bottle that I had lent to her back.

Mama said, "*Haibo,* Zowi! You guys should allow her to play with you and get her a doll to play with or share one of your toys with her".

"Mmm! I don't want to give her my toys," my sister started protesting on the other side. I don't know if the little girl thought my mother was talking to her, but she burst out crying and ran back and hid her face in the coloured woman's lap. Anyway, I felt like we didn't have much choice but to play with this girl. Our space had been invaded but we couldn't do much about it.

I think we were used to being just the two small kids at home. All the visitors who came to visit for a few days, or those boarders who came to stay and attend a local high school, were big. There was never a time when there was a child our age who came and disturbed our peace. I was crying, my sister Zitha was crying, and the girl was also crying. Meanwhile, my mother was promising us a bit of a hiding because, according to her, we were just being silly and unreasonable. Thembisa comforted the girl and looked in her purse and gave her sweets to give to us, so we ended up playing with her again. Mama was busy cooking this whole time.

Supper time came and we all sat around the big table in the kitchen with all the elders sitting on the red sofas that my mother owned. As things will go under normal circumstances, people were eating and chatting at the same time and Thembisa started sharing her thoughts.

"Aunty and uncle, like I said, I'm going to try and find a job here in the Eastern Cape, as one of my uncles used to own a supermarket in Umtata. The way I am so tired of struggling in Jozi, I want to go and check him to see if he could give me a job in his supermarket." She stressed her lack of interest in going back to Johannesburg as she had had it rough there for a while, due to unemployment. I don't think anybody really took this thought very far as she was just sharing what she was thinking without saying she was going to do it in a matter of a few hours to come.

I remember Mama asking her when the last time was that she had seen or talked to this uncle of hers. Thembisa answered and said that it had been years since they'd last spoken; before they ran away from home.

Mother: "Okay! Yhoo! So, you are not sure that this uncle is still there or not?"

Thembisa: "No, aunty. That's why I was thinking of going to Umtata tomorrow; to see if he's still there and if his business is still operational as well. I don't want to waste a lot of time, aunty."

Father: "That's great, but what is going to happen to your friend who you have brought with, if you find a job here in the Eastern Cape? Is she going back to Jozi?"

Thembisa: "No, no. We are going together, uncle. We are both going to look for jobs and work here in the Eastern Cape. I just pray we both find it. But I trust we will; if we can just find my uncle."

Mother came with a follow up question: "What are you going to do with the children?"

Thembisa: "Oh! The children, aunty? We are going to take them with us. We will go with them, aunty."

My parents were still listening to her when Jackie spoke in her big voice, emphasising what her friend had said. She said she would like to go with Thembisa as she was also looking for a job and she had the two kids to provide for.

The people in the house were probably thinking that Thembisa was going to say she would leave this woman friend of hers here at home and go find her uncle, then come back and maybe spend a couple of days and off they'd go to her own home, which was closer to Umtata. It would make common sense to go home and work from there. I want to think that my parents were of the idea that she was just visiting, just like she'd said, but was on her way home.

The idea that came from the big suitcases they had was that they came from Johannesburg straight to my place and I think Thembisa did imply that, even though not in so many words.

Alright! Time to sleep came and as usual we prayed and everybody went to their own space to sleep.

Day 3

The following day, everybody woke up as usual and we left for school and Mama left for work and the visitors were preparing to leave. They would go to Umtata and look for Thembisa's uncle and then go home to Reni, I supposed, or at least that's what everyone must have thought or understood to be case. I mean, Thembisa was an adult woman and no longer a teenager who wanted to run away from her mother's family anymore.

My family never really knew her home or her parents, or relatives for that matter. It was a matter of her and her brother Zwelibanzi having told my parents that their mother was from Reni and that made them to be from there as well. For example, I've met a lot of people in my journey of life and when a person tells me that they are from Dunoon, somewhere near Cape Town, and because of my familiarity with Cape Town and having an idea where Dunoon is, I start saying that particular person is from Dunoon Section 31, for example, without being sure about that. In this case, it was a matter of him telling my father that he was a Rhadebe, which happens to be our clan name. Also, he was from Reni and my father must have felt sorry for him as a young boy who was stranded and taken the story to tell his wife. They took his word for it and gave him a place to stay. A relationship was formed in that way, since the Mnyanis and the Rhadebes are the same people in terms of the clan.

That was the last time that we saw Thembisa and Jackie.

We came back from school and found my grandmother with the kids. *Haybo*! We thought they were leaving today, *mos*? Apparently, after everybody had left for school and work, Thembisa went to my grandmother and changed the story that she had sold to Mama and my father. They asked her to look after the kids for them for the day while they travelled to Umtata. My granny had been aware that they were leaving that day, and that they were taking their children with them. Hence, she was surprised when they asked her to mind the kids for them, but she agreed after being persuaded. They had promised to be quick; just in and out. Thembisa said they would go to see her uncle and come back immediately after that.

From my experience after I grew up and went to attend a high school in Umtata, I realised that going to Umtata and coming back from my place is a whole day's mission, especially if you don't have your own transport, which was the case with these two women. One has to take a taxi to Tsolo and from there take another one to Umtata and most of the time is spent at taxi ranks, waiting for the taxi to get full, so coming back "*now now*" was not to be. I'm just saying.

My mother was as surprised as us all when she came back and found the kids at home. By then we were starting to get used to them. The baby boy was just learning to stand using anything he could to stand, but mostly he crawled. I guess the love for them was starting to grow in our hearts as well. We waited for their parents to come back for them.

My whole family waited in anticipation to hear how the job search had gone. The evening went by and the night came without a sign of the two women. We looked up to the hill where the bus stop is, hoping they would appear, but nothing. Everybody at home was worried about them; about their well-being; the fact that they were not back and it was getting late; and the fact that Umtata was notoriously dangerous at times and they were like strangers in the area.

The baby was breastfeeding and there wasn't much food left for him. Actually, there was no food for him. My mother came up with something to feed him, just like she did for all of us. Fortunately, the boy was not particular when it came to food but he still missed his breast milk because he was crying and starting to be uncomfortable. The girl was also a bit moody as time went by. This was a confusing experience to us because, even though our home was always full of people coming and going, there had never been children our age or younger.

Eventually they fell asleep and still the two women were not back. Their mother, known to my family as Jackie, and her friend known as Thembisa, were gone – never coming back!

It became clear the following day that these women were not coming back when mama realised that they had actually taken one suitcase with them and only left one with the kid's clothes and their clinic cards.

There was no telephone at home so a telephone call from them was not expected. Maybe a telegram instead, or a letter, or a word or message given to a neighbour? It was quite possible to get hold of us, but nothing came forth. I saw my family's desperation as days went by, and weeks after that, and Thembisa and her friend were not seen or heard from. It meant that all of a sudden my mother, whose last born was five now, had a baby and that my grandmother, whose last born was in his forties, had small babies. It meant washing nappies, nursing a crying baby at night, worrying about what to feed this baby and all the added responsibilities of having a small baby in the house.

Word was put out for anyone with information on their whereabouts to contact my family, but it became clear that nothing and no one knew where they had been or what had happened to them.

We quickly had to adjust to having younger siblings. We soon had to realise that maybe they had planned to leave the children behind and never look back. Nothing whatsoever belonging to the two women was in that suitcase. The children had been born in Hillbrow in Gauteng, and their mother was Jackie – that was available from their clinic cards. Their names and surname were also available from their clinic cards.

Upon realising that these women were not coming back, the people in the community were as shocked as my family was. Some suggested that these could be my father's kids, since he'd once worked and stayed in Gauteng. People were just saying anything that would justify this incident of a woman leaving her children with strangers. Some would ask, why our home out of so many households in the village? I'm sure all of us would have loved to know the answer to that.... and some would say something didn't make sense or some would say something didn't add up or someone was not telling the truth. But, the truth of the matter is that we as people don't always have answers to everything that happens in our lives on this earth.

I want to think that somehow my family still had hope that Thembisa would come back for her friend's children and that there would be a proper explanation for the situation. It was not the first time that Thembisa had come to our place without being forced by anyone – she had come for her brother before, more than once – hence they waited a bit before alerting the authorities.

I must say, this was putting a lot of strain now on my granny and mom in terms of the needs of these two kids, especially the younger one. Soon, he was introduced to drinking tea as there was no milk and definitely no money to buy the milk. Other households in the village had cows they could milk, but that was not the case with my own home. My sister and I had long passed the stage of drinking milk; we basically ate whatever was on the menu for the day.

After a few days had passed without a trace of Thembisa and Jackie, a case was reported to the authorities and the chief in the village, but people somehow still believed that there could be an explanation for the disappearing act of these ladies. The fact that Thembisa was somehow related to my family, because she was a Rhadebe, seemed to pour water over the urgency or seriousness of the matter. My mother and granny decided to take the matter to the social services, but the officers who attended to them never took the matter seriously either. I remember my mother telling us how they were told to keep the kids and feed them with whatever she was feeding her own children. They said it was their gift and she should embrace it and raise the kids. How nice is that? Again they believed that she was related to these kids and that maybe the mother was going to show up eventually.

Days went by, nights went by, weeks, months, years and years went by, and no sign of the two women. My parents were left in disbelief, confusion and frustrated by this – in fact the whole family was – and I want to believe that the neighbours and the community were also confused by this.

As a believer, I know that there is someone who is the creator and author of our lives, and I believe that He writes the movie that we are all in and He makes changes as He sees fit, and He decides about all the characters featured in the movie... and I'll leave it at that. Some things one just doesn't have answers for.

Chapter 3

MONTHS WENT BY. MONTH AFTER month, the hope that someday maybe the mother would pitch lingered – but nothing. I don't want to imagine the anxiety the waiting and hoping brought to my mother and my grandmother; in fact to my entire family. Granny's only source of income was from a social grant which came every two months. My mother also had a small amount that she was getting from her job in the neighbourhood and as much as my father got from building other people's homes. Many of his clients failed to pay him on time and some recklessness also played a huge part in the resultant lack of things. Basically, that was all the income there was at home and my granny helped my mother and now there were two more small tummies to feed. The kids were left with Granny during the day, until everybody else came back in the afternoon.

Upon the discovery of their clinic cards, we started using the names that appeared on their clinic documents. The girl had two names on her card – Zona and an English name Dorcus – but her brother had only one name, which was Ande.

Granny suggested that the girl's hair be cut because she believed that it contributed to her being so skinny. In fact, even our hair would only be allowed to grow up to a certain point before my granny said the hair was either making us skinny or we didn't listen because of this long hair. We were used to that and, believe me, I know that it's crazy but it's true, and it's one of the things I still laugh about even now when I miss my granny. And, oh yes, the hair was cut and there she was, looking like us with a not so perfect brush cut, if I can call it that, as there were no hair clippers at home. They used to cut our hair with big scissors that were used to cut sheep's wool off. How do you like that, huh? I don't even know why they owned that kind of scissors as there were no sheep at home.

It wasn't too long after that, maybe a year or two, when a crèche opened in the community. All the kids in the village attended. I remember that it was some women from the village who took care of the kids at the crèche and taught them. It was the first time I had seen and heard of a crèche in my life. I hear a lot of people saying that there were crèches back then when they grew up and some people older than I am saying they had either attended a crèche or taken a sibling to the crèche, but for me it was the first time I'd heard about a crèche. I never attended anything like a crèche before attending school. Everything happened in school; I went through three different stages within one year in Sub A. Maybe that was our kind of crèche, without it being called a crèche. I want to believe that the crèche must have been free because, judging from the way things were so hard at home, my family could not have afforded to pay for it. The school fee at the primary school where my sister and I were attending was two Rand and sixty cents for each of us, and it would take a while before that could be paid.

My new siblings went to the crèche: both of them. Zona was forced to learn to speak IsiXhosa as no one spoke English there except her. Maybe at first it was very difficult for her, but she learned to speak it. If my memory serves me well, the crèche also helped her a lot with learning our language as they would sing a lot of songs and do recitations in IsiXhosa. It is true that it's more difficult for an adult to learn to speak a new language than it is for a child.

In a few years' time, we had to take Zona with us to school. My parents believed that she was big enough to start school, but Ande would continue attending the crèche. By the way, Zona was not so far from my sister in terms of age, maybe two years younger, but she was my sister's height. She was completely different from us, even after spending a couple years among us in the village.

I remember the first day we took her with us to school. I was in Standard 3 and my sister Zitha was probably in Standard 1. Back then at school all classes from Sub-A till Standard 1 shared a classroom, so Zona and my sister would sit in the same place, even though they were in different classes. We were also as good as newcomers in this school, as I had started when I was doing Standard 1, so we were still not so comfortable with everybody.

The first day we took Zona with us to school is one day I'll never forget in my life. Other kids at school were amazed, calling her *umlungu*, and the teachers were puzzled. She held onto me the whole time. I guess this was because, as much as the news of their arrival had travelled throughout the community, the school that we attended was not in the same village as my home so the kids from that side of town didn't know her. My own friends and neighbours from my community had already known her for quite some time, but it was only a handful of those kids who attended the same school as we did. Others attended other schools – either Ngxaza J. S. S. or Mabandla J. S. S. The teachers also didn't know anything about the story because the majority of them came from other villages.

She was dressed in navy blue nautical shorts, brown sandals and her navy blue cowl neck jersey, with long sleeves a bit big for her so that her arms and hands just disappeared in that jersey.

"*Yehake mntakaGeorge*," my teacher called out for everybody to hear. I knew that was it! That would be the beginning of a very long day for us in school that day. Couldn't she shut her mouth? I hated attention and I just wished I could run back home or escape this unnecessary attention. In my heart, God knows I was cursing everything; starting from the *tjatjarag* teacher, Zona, everybody at home who made me come to school with Zona, and myself. I wished I could be somebody else.

"Come here, Zowi *nana, nimfumana phi umlungu ngoku nana?* (where do you get umlungu now?) *Ngokabani lo mntana wena, Zowi?*(Whose child is this?) Hhee! Your father's things are always off-beat!" The teacher clapped her hands once more. The teachers kept on calling me and my two sisters and asking questions about the child and who her parents were, but I just told them that I didn't know who her parents were and that we'd brought her from home. I think that was an answer good enough from a nine-year-old.

Zona wouldn't remain in her class. She was just crying and not letting go of my dress and I was embarrassed and frustrated with her, and at the same time I was also confused. I know myself to be a very shy girl who usually avoids the spotlight, but I had nowhere to hide myself on that day. I kept on pulling my dress from her, asking her not to cry. I felt like I was drowning in this deep river and no one could see me and rescue me. I swore to myself I was not taking Zona to school again. When the school's bell rang signalling the end of the day I was not even in the mood to play. I was just tired and moody as well, so that we went straight home.

When we got back home I told my mother and granny how difficult my day had been and how I didn't want Zona to come with us to school as I couldn't even play at school because of all the hype around her and the attention she drew to us. Mama told me that it would get better as everyone got used to Zona, and that her staying at home because of that single bad day would only make things worse. People wouldn't get used to her and she would also not get used to a lot of people. She promised me that from then onwards things would only get better.

During the first few days at school, the teachers had to let her sit with me in my class. All that could be heard from my teacher were sighs, one after another. "*Umlungu*? *Hey hayi* Mondli's things are shocking everyday. Poor wife!" she said. Other teachers kept coming to my class and just standing at the door, having a conversation with my teacher, asking her how her new friends were doing. Those friends would be me and Zona, obviously, because they would be looking at us when they were talking. For some time, the issues that had befallen my parents were drawn into these conversations and some felt pity for us girls, my mom and granny, as the victims of whatever the situation they alleged was at play at home. As I sat there I was just anxious about what would happen the following day at school with my little sister Zona in the picture. Zitha was not a talkative person so it wasn't easy to know what her thoughts were on the matter and she didn't seem bothered by the drama of the day. I guess that was the beginning of our journey with them as our new siblings.

Everybody had to soon acquaint themselves with having responsibility for them. I found myself not having to mind my younger sister Zitha alone on the way to school, at school and back from school anymore as this little girl Zona would cling onto me. Zitha seemed not to mind this sudden takeover; she'd just grin sheepishly and I think even at home everybody had accepted their responsibility eventually. Everybody was doing their bit.

Zona looked terrified or rather overwhelmed by a lot of kids at school. I mean, there must have been less than ten children at the crèche. I guess because of her age it was her first exposure to a lot of people in one place at the same time.

Soon the extended family and family friends had to learn to understand the situation and accept these two kids as our own family. I remember when my cousins visited us during school holidays and it was the first time meeting my new siblings, it was difficult for them to understand where these two had come from. And from time to time I found myself having to caution them when they mistreated the younger girl, calling her *umlungu* or *ilawu* (which means coloured in my language). It was just a very odd thing to them to grasp this idea of us having a sister who was white all of a sudden but, when it came to an outsider, I somehow found myself standing up for and protecting Zona in the same way as I did for Zitha. I can't really remember how our local cousins reacted the first time we took our new siblings with us to attend a birthday party of one of my cousins. I guess the occasion didn't allow for people to notice the strangers. I carried the boy on my back, and walked with my two sisters.

Weeks, months and years went by without hearing from the two women who had brought the two kids into our lives; without anyone coming forward or claiming or alleging to have heard or seen them – not even by chance. Hopes were still there somehow, that the two women would come back and maybe have some explanation as to the reason for abandoning the children. There was a confusion at home as to what surname to use for Zona, now that she was attending school. The consensus was that both should use our surname in the interim and could always change if the status quo changed. So, there she was, Zona George, and I supposed the boy would be Ande George when his time to start school came.

They called my mother Mama just as we did. They didn't know more than that. I would assume that the girl might have missed her mom, but then again I guess she had forgotten. It's only now that I have kids of my own that I can imagine how sad and lonely she must have felt inside. I can't speak much about the boy in this regard because he was just too small to have known they had been left by their mom at some point. The mother he knew was my mother and the rest of my family he knew as his... at least that's what I thought but, like I said, I grew to have an idea of the reality that they must have faced inside, every day. We had accepted them as our blood siblings. I remember when we counted our siblings we would count them in, and the boy had assumed the position of last born at home; they had become part of us completely. My parents loved them and we loved them.

Ande was also growing up on the side, still attending the crèche. During the day, he would be at the crèche and after that my granny or my mother looked after him, depending on who was at home. Like I said earlier, there would always be somebody at home, either at my mother's or at my granny's. When we were home, we'd play *house* together but it was really difficult to play with Ande; he would just take everything and mess up our decorations. Zona would lose it and they'd end up fighting, with Ande crying for everything and Zona not wanting to play with him because he didn't listen. I sometimes became frustrated by all this. I mean, it's not like we didn't want to play with him because he was a boy. There were quite a number of boys we played with with those toys. It's just that Ande would cause everything to fall and, if one told him no, he'd cry.

There was one morning when my brothers killed a snake in the yard while they were busy cleaning it. It was a norm to clean the yard every weekend. My brothers would collect all the rubbish. Tins would be put to the side, but all the papers and plastic bottles would be burned together with fabric stuff before they took all the tins to a nearby dumping place. It was the same situation on this morning and we girls, together with Mama, were preparing to go to the nearby river to do our laundry. My brothers were cleaning the yard when they were confronted by a snake. There was a noise. Before I could understand what the noise was about, they had managed to kill the snake. In the meantime, the rubbish was burning at the far end of the yard. Upon killing the snake, they decided to throw it in the fire and burn it with the rubbish. Everybody by that time was awake, including Ande. If I have to estimate his age at the time, I'd say that he was probably around three years old.

He was walking about in the yard when all this was happening and, when the snake was put in that fire, he was there watching and trying to talk to my brothers, but no one could make out his speech at that time. He took quite a long time before he could speak properly, I must say, although I don't know what the problem was.

Ande just stood there watching while the snake burned and we left for the river to do the laundry. When we came back to hang some of the washing up, he was sitting by that same fire, even though the fire had died down. But now one could see that he'd been eating something and his face was just shining, as if he just had fish and chips or something.

"What's that one doing sitting there?" I asked curiously.

"He looks like he's been eating something," Zona suggested. "Look at his cheeks, sisi. *Hey wena*! What are you eating there?" I asked

He pointed at the fire, saying his own thing that no one could understand. My mom asked him what he was eating and one of my brothers went closer, only to realise that he had blisters on his hands from removing the snake from the fire and eating it. I know, right? Plus, a piece of the burnt snake was still in his hand. That's the day he scored himself a nickname from my brothers. They named him *Sgwili*, a word used to refer to a wealthy person. There is a belief or myth amongst Africans that if one eats a snake one will be brave or wealthy. Everybody was laughing at the boy and praising him for his bravery and courage for removing the burning snake from the fire and helping himself to it.

As the time went by, Zona and I became very close. At home, it was a norm that if a person was older than you it's a must that you respect that person and you do that by not calling them just by their name. It was like that for my older brothers as well as for the other relatives and even strangers: if a person is older than you are, you can't call them just by their names. So they were taught to call me sisi. I became sisi alone to them, and my sister Zitha became sisi-Zitha.

We fetched water together from the river. I would carry a five-litre bucket and my two sisters would carry a two-litre container of water each. We washed and cleaned the house together and we also fetched wood from the bush to make fire, together with my grandmother, even if it meant that some of us would carry one piece or drag a small branch only.

As the years went by, the kids grew as well. There was a time they both fell ill and it later turned out to be a chicken pox and it affected only the two of them. Zona was really sick before the symptoms of chicken pox came out. I remember my mother was already working in town and we were left with my grandmother and, because Granny was already old, I had to carry Zona on my back to the clinic to get the medical attention that she needed.

I had a best friend in the village called Zozo and she helped me carry Zona all the way to the clinic and back. Under normal circumstances, one would be given aloe or salt water to drink if one were sick, but her temperature was just too high and it wouldn't drop and she was becoming weak. Also, she started to talk in her sleep so my granny suggested that we go to the clinic. Ande didn't have a high temperature, but the infection became visible as he had blisters on his body, especially around his waist. Zona was given a soap to use in the bath and some syrup to drink by the nurse who saw her.

Anyway, like any other children, they both recovered in no time and everything was back to normal.

Our bonds grew and became stronger each day because she was a sweet girl – loud, jolly and always ready to join the fight. As she grew up, she became this wonderful person day by day. By this time we were sleeping at my granny's house. We still did everything else at my mom's, but we slept on the other side. Zona and I shared a bed. I liked her a lot already. I am sure that we had some common traits; being loud, jolly and a bit mischievousness.

∘∘∘∘∘ **Chapter 4** ∘∘∘∘∘

THERE WERE A NUMBER OF times that we got into trouble because of her love for animals. I found myself falling for all these funny things of hers; like sneaking Box's puppies inside my granny's house because she couldn't stand seeing them on the veranda in the cold, especially in winter. We would sneak them inside the house and place them under our blankets, thinking that my granny was sleeping and wouldn't know, forgetting that she was the first one to wake up in the morning. But it was not even a matter of Granny waking up in the morning and finding the puppies inside the house in our blankets; it was the puppies making a noise when they started feeling too warm. Many times we got a hiding for those puppies and many other things in which she was instrumental. I would hate her for it, but when she asked me with concern to help these small creatures, I would do it again and again. It was just difficult to hate her for long and, no mistake, Zona was naughty, period.

We had a cat at home that she loved very much and as I shared a bed with her the cat would sleep on our feet because she'd call it and kiss it and talk to it. I must admit that at first I found that behaviour very strange, but I got used to it after some time. That was my crazy sister, Zona. She was very short-tempered, but also very loving and sweet. It didn't matter whether she knew a person or not.

There were many occasions where we would find other kids fighting and all of a sudden she would join the fight. What was a bit embarrassing was that while fighting she'd be lamenting and making a noise, helping whoever seemed to be losing the fight or seemed to be bullied. These fights were not even hers and I used to not understand her. Later I realised that she didn't tolerate bullying, and as you know there are always those children who enjoy bullying others after school, regardless of their gender. In many instances I also found myself having to fight after school just because so and so said so. This was annoying for me because I was a coward, but most of the times one didn't have a choice but to fight because, even if one didn't want to fight the opponent would bully you just to show off and one would just be their daily bread and they would prepare you in front of their friends and enemies, every day.

With Zona, it didn't matter who was fighting – she would get into that fight. I must confess that I hated that because it meant that sometimes I could end up getting involved in the fight myself. I had a few of my haters of whom I was pretty much scared, but when things broke loose and a challenge was there for me to fight – and sometimes in cases where I would have asked my feet to carry me home safely instead – there she would be, cheeky and not scared of anything.

This reminded me of my biological sister Zitha; that one was also not scared of anything or anyone but the difference between the two of them was that my Zitha didn't talk too much or make a noise. She would say one word and you'd never hear her again. But Zona could talk! *Shame*, she had a big mouth.

I remember one time I found myself involved in some fight that I would have avoided if she had not been there. I was scared of my opponent because in her family everybody, including even the dog, would come out if a person beat or fought with their child, boy or girl. And these people were plus sizes and, yhoo, they could shout. I ended up fighting with this girl while we were at the river to fetch water and, guess what? I was bitten on my cheek and, even though the fight had happened on a Saturday, it meant that I had a pretty big scar on my face and I had some explaining to do when I got to school on Monday. I had to flee from my home and run to the rocks up the hill to escape the wrath of that girl's family for a while. There was no one at home besides us, as Granny had gone somewhere. I mean, I was punished again at school for the same fight and for having a stupid mark in my face. It was embarrassing. Zona had done the same nonsense that she always did, not staying out of unnecessary trouble.

After some time we learnt to understand her. We would ask her and tease her about her behaviour and everybody would laugh about it, including her, but if a fight broke out again, she'd be in on it again.

On weekends, especially Saturdays, we would go to the river together to do our washing. This meant waking up early in the morning, collecting all our dirty laundry, putting it in those big zinc buckets and rushing to the river to try and avoid the long queues. Remember that on Saturdays everybody had a chance to wash their clothes and in my village there were a lot of boarders who attended a local high school and there were only two rivers. The one closer to my home was easily accessible and therefore preferable to most people. So, if you slept late, chances are you would spend almost half of your Saturday at the river because of waiting in the queue for your turn to get water to actually get started with your washing.

Doing the washing on Sunday was not allowed at home. On Sundays we would go to church with Granny. The church was next to our school. My granny would wake us up early on Sunday to prepare for church so that we could leave the house early enough to make it on time for the service. The four of us – Zitha, Zona, Ande and I – would leave first and my granny would follow behind. From time to time, Ande would protest and I would have to pick him up or carry him on my back. I could understand that the distance was just too much, and besides I was the big sister.

The boy had this routine that he had before he could sleep. He would roll his head on his pillow made with his jersey while lying on his back and sing a song that sounded like all our names as his siblings and sometimes the song would involve *Makhulu* (Granny) and Mama as well. I think this was just his own lullaby that helped him to sleep. He slept on a mattress on the floor alone, as there were only two beds in my granny's place. Anyway, we also slept on the floor sometimes when it thundered and this was no big deal.

He grew up with the nickname *Sgwili*, and everybody called him that – at home and in the village as a whole. By the way, we all had silly nicknames that were given to each of us, either because of how we looked or something stupid that we'd done, but I can promise you it was always an ugly and undesirable name. Some of us managed to keep our silly nicknames under wraps, but for our juniors it was not that easy. Zona's nickname, because of her character, had something to do with gossiping, but she accepted it and responded well when we called her *Mamgobhozi*.

If they went somewhere where I didn't, I had no worries because she and Ande would come back and act everything out for me and my granny, word by word and action by action. We'd laugh until our tummies couldn't take it anymore. Sometimes my grandmother would try to talk us out of it, because sometimes they would imitate even people from church; how they sang and their actions in church, but we'd just move from where Granny was and go somewhere else to continue with our noise and laughter.

They were just two happy and playful kids. Zona could sing and act. I just loved them. Many times we got into trouble, with Granny pinching us, because we played or laughed during prayer before we went to bed. Sometimes we'd set each other up; we'd come up with silly rules before prayer just to set each other up so we could laugh about it.

Their strange arrival was known in the wider community and people in the community would donate clothing items and shoes to them from time to time. Some would express their disappointment at the social workers for not taking the issue seriously and assisting with the two kids. I never understood what kind of assistance the so-called social workers could give in that situation. In my own mind, I seriously thought the social workers were supposed to find the mother of these two and that they refused. At some point I even wanted to become a social worker when I grew up; one who did her job, though. I promise, *I* would have found those two women.

There were times when they would be troublesome and would just fight among themselves. When they started with that nonsense I would be so irritated because it meant there would be wailing and screaming the whole time. Ande would cry and Zona would wail and scream to the extent that my granny would sometimes get up from her bed, get a stick and separate them.

I later realised that at times it was a pretence fight, just to tease my granny because they knew that she would react. You would hear wails and screams and think that they were fighting, but when you got there they'd just laugh at you. That's how crazy they could be.

It was a pleasure growing up with them. I sometimes wonder how life would have turned out for me if they hadn't been there; with my parents separating and Zitha leaving to stay with my maternal granny, and my older brothers having left for Cape Town. I would have easily been the only child at home, besides my one older brother who came back from staying with some relative in Mqanduli in another part of the Eastern Cape.

I must say that, besides an ear problem that used to keep me away from school quite a number of times, I don't remember being a sickly child. I can't say the same about these two. Zona was a sickly child. It was easy for her to catch a fever, or have a temperature, headache, stomach ache, you name it – but nothing serious. I had to take her to the clinic on a number of occasions and she would be fine again. The only serious illness I remember Ande having was the chicken pox that surrounded his waist area and maybe a stomach bug here and there, but that's all. He was a strong boy who loved his food and that's the only problem we as his sisters had with him. He just didn't know when to stop eating and at night you'd hear him moaning, wanting to go outside to relieve himself.

"Jeez! Sgwili! Who wants to go outside in the middle of the night?" For heaven's sake, even if it was not in the middle of the night, I hated it with my all. Remember I said that I'm not the bravest of them all, so I avoided anything that would keep me outside in the dark. The mood outside at night would just feel so creepy to me, like there was something that was going to catch me. If it were not too dark, there would be a full moon and there'd be crickets and frogs singing and here and there you'd see a small light moving from one place to another. In my mind, all those were ghosts or things of the night that were looking to catch me and I was really scared of them.

Once you heard that sound coming from his mattress on the floor you just wanted to disappear into your bed because the next thing to follow was either him calling, "Sisi, sisi, please accompany me. I need to go outside; I'm pressed," in a voice already making one feel guilty. Plus, who wanted him to mess inside the room? How were we going to sleep if he did?

Or it would be Granny calling me, "Zowi, *mkhapheni aye phandle umntana, nimse pha emva kwendlu azokwazi ukuzinceda, utya gqithi nawe man kwedini*".

Yho! Ndafa Nkosi! I felt like saying that, with tears welling up in my eyes. Of course, I couldn't say that to my grandmother so instead I'd jump out of bed and throw my blankets aside with anger and curse inside, while Zona could not hide her own emotions. She'd be giving it to him and even pushing him.

"Come, come, come, you are boring man. We must not sleep because of your greed... yhe? We must be waking up and going outside at night because, *wena,* you can't control yourself?"

"The problem is that this thing becomes a routine, so you must practise to keep it till morning, brother, like all of us," I'd be adding on the side. Because I was so uncomfortable in the dark, if I ever needed to relieve myself at night nothing would come out, even if I had someone to watch me. Anyway, we'd rush him to *make quick* so we could get back to the house and when he finally finished, nhe! The race to that door, nhe! No one wanted to be the last one to enter the house. I don't know whether they were scared too, or if I had managed to instil fear in them because of my own phobia of the dark.

Back then, there was no electricity in the village so if it was night and there was no moon, then one couldn't even see one's own legs. It would be worse when it was misty. Funnily enough, I used to think I was scared of the dark and somehow these two were also scared of the dark, or whatever they were scared of, because of me. I later realised that it was not necessarily the dark I was afraid of. I remember a few times when it was clear outside because of the moon and I'd still be scared of my own shadow.

There was a night that took the crown of all those crazy nights. We were coming from my mom's house as usual, and we were already on our marks, ready to sprint to my granny's house and for some reason my shadow was in front of me. I was with these two and I was carrying something to eat for granny. Hey! I don't know what came into my mind but I got a fright from seeing this shadow and I started running. I guess Ande thought maybe there was something chasing us and he started crying loudly. Zona started running as well and while running I tripped over my leg and flew to the ground. I don't even want to think about the food I was carrying. Mamgo tripped on top of me and Sgwili tripped also; we were all on the ground and yha! a bit confused. I had taken a bit of a knock, but we got up and took off again and when we got to Granny's house we were all crying and full of dust. I was bleeding on one knee and had no food with me. Those plates had been left there for whatever we were running from to keep.

My granny just looked at us and said, "You kids behave like you are not alright upstairs. There's nothing that has ever eaten anyone in this yard and certainly it won't start with such ugly people." We knew that night that we were ugly, but I still wouldn't risk it, even if I were ugly. Sitting there, trying to nurse my bruised knee and elbows, I tried reflecting on what had happened out there and I realised that it was that damn shadow that must have led to all that mess. These kids wouldn't have run if I hadn't, so really, maybe I was the one who scared them.

Sometimes our granny would go away on church conferences in Somerville, another location that still fell under Tsolo district, where the Headquarters for her church was, and we'd be left alone at home and we would have to take care of the pigs, chickens and the dogs – and the cat, of course. You'd never forget the cat because of Mamgo. Sometimes we'd have to close the door because it was becoming dark at night and the cat would be outside. Mamgo would literally stand at the door and be calling the cat to come back to the house. I was not that crazy about cats and dogs; if it was not inside it could sleep wherever it happened to be if left up to me.

It got to a stage where I was the one who cooked for the family. My granny was getting old and she would rest, especially when the weather was bad. Mamgo and I would have to get wood and I'd prepare the food for all of us. Some days were bad, when the pap wouldn't be well-cooked you know, and what I liked about these two is that they'd make me laugh about it, even if I'd get talked to or was given a hiding. I gradually learned to cook the pap, steam bread, stamp and sometimes *iinkobe* (mealies). Those were the serious foods that were mostly cooked at home. I struggled a lot at first because sometimes the fire wouldn't be enough and the food wouldn't be well cooked, especially pap and steam bread, and sometimes it would be too much and I'd burn the food.

On rainy days we'd sit around the fire and cook in a small flat that had been built for such purposes. Sitting there on our own, cooking and playing on the side, we'd play *the in-laws*. All three of us would be in-laws to each other and we'd imitate how all the people we knew used to talk to each other, including my own father. The room was filled with wood and kindling and all the things that would enable one to quickly start a fire. We'd pretend to be smoking and drinking *umqombothi*, the traditional beer and just talk nonsense to each other. I slowly allowed Zona to cook with me, especially things like the soup and potatoes.

They were doing well in school and at church as well. I used to feel for them, even though they never showed any signs of not being content with the parents they now had, who were my own parents. My grandmother had made sure that they attended the Sunday school and were part of the kids' ministry at church.

○○○○○ **Chapter 5** ○○○○○

THE YEARS WENT BY VERY fast and seven years later, when I had finished Standard 7, as we called it then, I left the village to go and attend the high school in Umtata. Henceforth, I would go home only during school holidays. This was because home was a bit far and there were financial constraints. I had mixed feelings about the whole situation of leaving my home to stay in Umtata; I was excited and sad at the same time. My granny was getting very old and, though Mamgo was well groomed to clean and cook, she was still a very young girl of only ten or eleven years old. My granny was by no means dependent on anyone; she could still pretty much take care of herself and us too. It was just that I felt like I was also abandoning them.

My granny was elated by my progress and she believed I would grow up and become something big in society. She used to tell me that I'm bright, whatever that meant. Zona and Ande didn't really show any emotions about the move. I think they understood the idea of people leaving home to board in another place when they get to high school. They could see a lot of students from different places boarding in our village, including our home at times. Another thing was that Zona knew that some of my friends were also going to attend high school in Umtata. She knew a lot of my stuff, my friends, what I got up to as a teen. I mean that girl was curious; her nickname was not a mistake.

The first holiday came and I went home. Nothing was different there. We stayed up almost the whole night getting updates from my recorder, Mamgo, about school, village, river, church, the fights and all that had gone down during the few months I'd been away. Ande was no different, and he would even show me the actions of what had happened so that I'd have a proper idea. They would fight for turns to gossip.

When the time to go back to school came, they would walk me to the bus stop and wait with me there until I got a taxi. I remember my brother Ande would say, "Sisi, only the best, nhe!" meaning there would be taxis that we'd let pass because he didn't want his sister to catch a *skorokoro*. He'd say, "Hayi sisi, this one *iyakhohlela* and you can see also that it doesn't have a shape anymore," meaning that it was coughing. We didn't have a car at home; the Datsun bakkie that used to belong to my father was no more, even way before they came. We'd stay at Adonis bus stop, making fun of all the cars and taxis that passed until there was no time to play anymore and I really had to go.

Everything continued to be okay, I suppose, until the second year in Umtata when I was in Grade 11. When I went home for the June holidays I found everyone at home besides Ande; he had gone to play with his friends. It was a good feeling being home but I sensed some dull atmosphere. Zona was not so excited to see me and she couldn't hide her foul mood. I suspected that maybe she was angry about something and that she'd be fine in no time, as she usually was, so after a few moments of being confused by the behaviour I decided to leave her alone. Since Ande was not there, and my favourite radio Mamgo was not playing, so I decided to take a nap.

Late in the evening, after I had made food for everyone, Mamgo called me to the side. "Sisi, can I ask you something?"

"Okay, she's fine now, finally." I tried to get her to crack a smile, but it wasn't there.

"Come on, baby girl, let's talk. What's eating you so much that you don't look even excited anymore when your big sis is back? What's happened?" I was beginning to worry now and, looking at her, I just saw tears welling up in her big eyes.

Zona: "Sisi, there's something that I want to ask you about, it's bothering me. People are saying that our parents are actually not Sgwili's and my biological parents. Also, that makes you guys not to be our biological siblings."

Me: "Hayibo! Who is saying that to you?" I reacted quite upset with whomever was making this issue theirs and, to be honest, I had almost forgotten that they were not my biological siblings.

Zona: "This has been on the ground for some time now, but I used to ignore it and now what is bothering me is that even here at home that's what people are saying."

Me: "Hayibo! You are lying! Who are those people, Zona?" I lamented

Zona: "A lot has been happening here, sisi, since you left; we have been asked to change our surname from the one we know to another alleged surname of ours. Are these things true, sisi? Are we not your real siblings, *kanti*?"

She asked me that question looking me straight in the eye, with her eyes full of tears. All this while I was holding my peace, gutted, not sure of what to say to her and hoping that she was going to identify the culprit to be someone who was not my family, someone whom it would be easy for me to call to order. But she had mentioned that even people here at home… I was flat, feeling a big lump in my throat as if I was choking on something.

Zona: "It's not like one is being disrespectful but I feel so confused and angry at the same time because I… I don't under… I don't understand this, sisi. No one is giving me a proper explanation as to how and why this is happening now in our life." She sobbed… a whole lot.

Me: "Shh! Shh! Mamgo, I'm so sorry." Tears started rolling down my cheeks and I pulled her to me and I gave her a hug. I kept her there, holding her tight. "I'm really sorry. I really don't know what to say to you and my heart is broken to see you like this. Please tell me what happened and how we got here… what is going on here at home, *kanti*? Who told you that we are not blood siblings?"

Zona: "*We,*" she sniffled. "A few months ago we were taken to the social workers because Sis'Nomandla felt that we were growing and that Granny could do with some extra financial assistance for us since we were only living on her social grant and our needs were becoming more…." More sniffles. "She felt that it was only correct that we get a social grant and it was when we went to see the social workers that I heard about the issue of a different surname. They said our surname is not George. Sisi! Can you believe it? Is it true, sisi?"

Me: "Owh, my God! What the hell? Who was there with you? I mean who took you there?"

Zona: Sniffles again. "They said something about our birth certificates that had to be applied for first and that our real surname would be used to apply for such before we could get to apply for a social grant."

Me: "What the hell? Who said you needed birth certificates? As big as I am, I don't have a birth certificate; that's absolute madness! You know that I used to play sports at school using my cousin's birth certificate *mos*... I mean just yesterday... here in front of you," I lamented. I was cursing the social worker, Sis'Nomandla, my aunt who had accompanied these kids to the social worker, the social grant and everything. I was cursing the social workers firstly for refusing to find the mother of these kids initially (according to my understanding of their job) and secondly for messing up with them again.

Zona: "They said we have to change our surname and use our correct and official surname going forward and, and, sisi, I don't want this surname, I don't want to change my surname to some surname I don't know."

Me: "Believe me, you don't have to, Mamgo. No one can force you to use it if you don't want to."

Zona: "If we were not born by the same parents as you guys, then who's our mother and father and where are they, sisi?"

Me: "I don't know, Mamgo. I'm so sorry. I wish I knew all these things you are asking me," I sniffled. My tears were just running down my face straight onto her hair, since I was still holding her with my chin resting on her head. I brushed her arm with my right hand. My holiday, which I had been so looking forward to, had just started with a bang. One big mess had happened. I could feel my stomach cringe from the fear of the uncertainty of what this thing was bringing to my whole family and these two kids; from the fear that their lives could change forever.

Zona: "This whole thing feels like one big secret affair. Why were we not told all along? Sisi!" She freed herself from my hug and pushed me a little. She looked at me, her face enveloped with desperation and asked slowly, "*Sisi wam*, did you know something all along? Why didn't you say anything?"

Oh heavens! What was I going to say to this girl? I battled to control my tears and what truly broke me was that I knew their reality – our reality. I knew that eventually people would start telling them on the side. I just didn't, in my little mind, think my family, especially my granny, was ready for that. At the same time, I hadn't really got worried that they would find out eventually because it never occurred to me that there would be a situation that would need that ugly reality to be unveiled so roughly, probably because I was aware of the attempt that was made by my family to report their situation to the social workers upon realising that their parents were not coming back. I was sure that the social workers had made their decision and they were not interested in finding their mother.

To my mind, finding out would occur with their mother coming back and being introduced to them. I never thought that they would find out their identity and at the same time not have a substitute parent; it was supposed to be like a perfect handover. Something like, "Look kids, this is not your real family but this is your mother," kind of thing. Also, it had never occurred to me that at some point they would have to go through being forced to change their identity or surname. I guess I was just a child having fairy tale of thoughts, or a confused child with confused thoughts.

My heart broke into pieces when I saw the hurt in her eyes. "Come here, let's sit down," I said to her, pointing to the bed. "Everything will be fine, I promise. Look, I'm still your best sister, no matter who says what. Surname or no surname, I still love you so much.

"This doesn't change anything, I promise you. Much as I knew something about this, I don't think it was my place as a child to say it, plus those same people who brought this upon you now are the very people who were not interested when this matter was taken to them initially. You have to understand that whatever my family did was out of love for you and Ande. They did what they thought was

 A Journey from Nowhere to Nowhere

right by reporting the issue to the authorities, including the social services, but were turned away. What they had left was to raise you guys and protect you from the things that they themselves could not understand.

"Wait a minute! What I am trying to say here is don't rush to take this and run with it without understanding all the sides of the story. I know that it's going to be difficult to trust anything now, but I plead with you, Mamgo. I might not know everything about this, but I know that my family would not have wasted their time, if you want to call it that, to accept you guys and raise you if they didn't love you. We honestly do. If anything happened here it was love."

I was now crying and just saying anything that came to mind. "But look, listen, how about this? Tomorrow I will speak to my grandma to find out what is happening?" I suggested in a pleading way. She could only nod her head in agreement with me. Her already big eyes were even bigger because of crying and her nose was congested. A very cold mood filled the room. I was full already. I was not going to be able to eat the food that I had prepared. I felt the sound coming from my tummy that things were not alright anymore at home.

The following day I made time to speak to my grandma and she explained to me that they were trying to apply for a foster care grant for them and the social development had requested their documents. By their documents it was understood to have meant their clinic cards since they were the only documents available as part of their belongings in that huge suitcase they were left with. That's where their surnames were recorded. My family had never given them new first names, besides their crazy nicknames, of course, although they carried our surname. Well, this information was not new to me at all; I knew all that.

My granny told me that this issue pained her because she could see how it was affecting the two kids and she regretted the results that had been produced by this application for the foster care grant. So, basically, that was how my siblings got the official confrontation about their true identity; a faceless mother, a fake home, a village they thought they belonged to, fake parents, fake siblings. Only the two of them had something in common. The home they had known for all their lives was just not what they'd thought it was.

Me: "Granny, what made Sis'Nomandla come with all this now?" I asked with some sense of annoyance, because I still believed that people like getting involved in other people's business. I thought it was just another stunt of someone trying to get information, just to gossip about it. As much as we were not allowed to swear, especially in front of old people, I swear that my heart was swearing at and cursing all those involved in bringing misery to my little siblings. And I had to be careful in my choice of words; being in high school didn't mean I could now question old people.

Granny: "*Ey! Zowi, andithi ebesithi uyanceda ngelakhe mntanam?" Akukho nomnye umntu ebekhe wacinga ukuba izophuma kulendawo yonke lento. Lonto indivisa kabuhlungu ngoku yonke lento.*"

Me: "I understand, Ma! I know that you and everybody else meant well."

All she wanted for them was the best. She'd agreed to apply for the grant because she was old and felt that anything could happen to her anytime. And, because Sis'Nomandla was educated and well respected in the society, when she showed interest in such a low family as my family, especially with both my granny's and the two kids' interests at heart, her advice was well received. It was true that my granny was in her early eighties and her social grant wouldn't be able to take care of the needs of teenagers forever. So, everybody thought that it would be proper if they could be taken care of, like any adopted or foster care kids, by the social services.

My granny was not a person who showed weakness or emotions, even in difficult situations, but I knew her. I could hear her disappointment in her big yet calm voice. She knew that her social grant was not enough for them anymore. She was aware that these two were also growing and their needs were becoming more and more; if it was not this that is needed for school by Ande then it would be Zona looking for that.

She repeated what my little sister had said to me the previous night: that she did not want to change her surname and that she'd cried a lot since this thing had come up. She said that she had received reports from the school that the kids were being somewhat rebellious towards their teachers and peers.

Me: "So, *sizokwenza njani ke xa kunje, Makhulu?*" I asked.

Granny: "There's nothing much, my child. This is still so new to them. After a while they will get used to it and it will get better."

Me: "Maybe, they can be allowed to continue using our surname until they are comfortable with this new information and surname? Just maybe, *Makhulu?*" I asked again.

Granny: "Well, I don't know if that would help them in any way, my child."

Me: "Because it's almost as if we are also throwing them away now," I interjected. "The sense that I am getting is that they feel like the family also doesn't want them to use our surname anymore. It's like we are saying to them, 'Here, this is your new identity and from now on you are no longer allowed to use our surname because you have yours'. I apologise for cutting you short, Granny, but don't you think?"

She promised to give it some thought and maybe talk to some other family members to understand the potential consequences that this could have, especially on official documents, because the girl would soon be going to a high school which would be a completely new environment with people who wouldn't have her background information.

I was disappointed but took comfort in the fact that my granny was willing to consider and consult other people at home; people like my father and probably brother as well. I don't know up till today how I would have handled the discovery, if it had been me in their shoes. I took pride in who I was, even though I was poor. My family meant the world to me. I'm a sucker for my family; for my siblings. To wake up one day and be told an otherwise story would destroy me.

I didn't blame my family at all for anything. They were not the ones who had messed up. All they had done was to receive children who were dumped with them and raise them with love. It was not going to help to point fingers at that stage. Besides, the woman who deserved to be fingered was nowhere to be found. I could strangle Jackie for all this pain, I tell you. I prayed to God to help us; to see us through, as the pain was just too much. I was hurt, but I think my granny was hurt even more and that Zona and Ande were hurt the most.

Some things are just unfair. I remembered what people had said when these kids first arrived at my home, all the questions that everybody had, and I realised that even at that point we had not found answers to those questions. Instead, more questions had accumulated. I had to beg God to bring Jackie back; at least that would be a bitter-sweet situation for my baby sister and brother. But, like I said earlier in the book, I believe that there is a creator who writes this movie called life. He changes the characters as He sees fit and the script goes the way He wants it to go. Perhaps my request was not part of the script and Jackie's comeback was not part of the movie.

⸰⸰⸰⸰⸰ **Chapter 6** ⸰⸰⸰⸰⸰

I WAS UPSET AND HELPLESS. MY school holidays were just spoilt and nothing was interesting anymore. The usually bubbly person who would gossip and update me with all the events that had taken place in my neighbourhood while I was away was spending most of her time sleeping. She was not interested in anything. Why did they have to face this again? Wasn't the first blow of being abandoned by their mother big enough already? How must they be feeling now? Disappointed, hurt, betrayed, lied to – a whole lot of things must be running through their minds. Those were the kinds of questions that kept on going through my head.

At least Zona had shared some of her feelings with me. It was extremely difficult for her to process it all. I mean, it was difficult enough for me to live without my mother, even though I knew that she was in Cape Town, trying to work for me, so my siblings' burden weighed very heavily on me as well. Ande was not engaging much about the issue at hand. He just told me that they knew that they didn't belong with us. Some people had been telling them that they had been left by their mom at our home when they were very small. Immediately I could sense the distance between me and my younger brother. He was still very young and tender, but clearly broken. He was somehow very cheeky and back chatting and didn't care much about anything anymore.

In a few days, my grandma called us and told us that it was okay, they could continue using our surname at school. Just so long as / Zona knew that her official things would reflect her real surname, we had a deal. You should have seen the big smile on her face… it just melted my heart.

My holidays ended and I had to go back to school and, as usual, my sister walked with me to the bus stop and we were back to the way things were before the surname and *identity scandal* broke out.

That year I went to visit my mother and my siblings in Cape Town during the December school holidays and I didn't get a chance to hear of all the developments after I'd left for school the previous time. Staying in boarding school, I learned that I was not the only child who struggled financially; some learners used to go home very often, like every other week. They did not have to wait for holidays before they could go home, but I soon realised that it was not only me who had to wait for such a long time before I could go back to my village; to my home; to my people and my friends whom I had left behind. The school would make it compulsory to go home during the long holidays – the June and December holidays – but were lenient during short breaks like March and September. I was one of those who remained behind during those short breaks.

When the time came for the schools to open in January, it was time for me to go back home in preparation for going back to Umtata. The day I arrived at home I saw different people; my younger sister Zona had lost weight, quite significantly. Though she was not sick or feeling any pain, she looked like she was. There was excitement when I arrived, with Zona teasing and trying to pick me up sometimes, trying to measure her height against mine. My granny was excited to have me back as always. Owh! She loved meat and the first thing she

     A Journey from Nowhere to Nowhere

asked, after asking how I was of course, was whether her daughter-in-law had sent some *amaroco* (chickens) from Cape Town with me and, believe me, all those chickens that Mama had sent with me to my granny as *umphako* had to be cut into pieces, placed in a black pot and cooked there and then.

Okay, maybe if we'd had a refrigerator it would have been a different story. My baby brother Ande was there. He was excited to have his sisi back and, of course, excited about the gifts – and I must not forget the meat. I don't want to mention the fact that back then we used to get super excited and happy when there was meat in the menu. It was a luxury and didn't happen all the time. It was a sure case that we'd eat meat when granny got paid her social grant, but any other meat days would be a bonus; hence the excitement.

Later in the day, I had a chat with Zona and Ande and we were teasing her about the bones that were showing all over her body and she just laughed at me. Ande even teased that the oil from the chickens should be given to Zona to drink so it could nourish those pokey bones. Along the way I asked how they were doing and if they had done well in school in the previous year. I was boasting that I was going to Standard 10. Zona indicated that they were actually doing well; the wind and the storm had blown over, she had passed but her brother had failed.

Me: "Awu! This one has failed? Brother! And then?"

Zona: "Speak for yourself, *wena*! I'm not your spokesperson. You are clever, *mos*, and you can see the pokey bones, but you don't…"

Ande interjects: "Oh! I thought I should give you the platform so you could finish, since you were so fast to tell sisi that I have failed. *Nx! Uyaphapha* man! That's the problem."

Zona: "*Aysuka*! Answer the question that sisi has asked you, *Ngqina*, and leave me alone."

Ande: "Hhee! Yho! You are like that now? This is you? Sharp Ngqina,
    sharp nomD.
Me: "Haibo! Guys, what's up *kanti*? I still"
Zona: interjecting before I could finish what I wanted to say. "No,
    sisi, this one must not beat about the bush. Come out, *bhuti*.
    Answer *mos*. The question stands"
Ande just burst out laughing: "I can't believe it's you who's putting
me in the frying pan like that, *mos*. One minute, sisi is here and you
want to shine? You are unbelievable you know, *Mamgo*."
Zona: "Okay, okay. Sisi, since I'm being accused of trying to shine
    because of you, let's forgive the dude, let's leave him."
We all laughed and I agreed to let it go, temporarily.
Me: "I'm happy that we can all laugh together again, guys. The last
    time we saw each other was a very bad experience in my life.
    I have missed you and your craziness."
Zona: "Ewe, Sis'wam, it was a terrible period for us too. I can say
    that I'm still battling with getting used to the change because
    it still makes me angry. I just can't get used to any of it. I just
    don't know the person I see in the mirror and sometimes it
    becomes better if I cautiously look for the old self. Really, sisi,
    who do I say I am?"
I'm sure that everyone is aware that the teachers at school usually
use a surname to call a learner and this didn't make things any better
for these two kids. One almost wasn't sure which one would be more
sensitive to the situation: to call them by George or to call them
Mdledle. Either would remind them of the status quo. This was
echoed by Ande; that it was tough because he didn't know how to
feel when being called by either of the two surnames.

Ande jokingly detailed instances where he just didn't respond to
the teacher when being called with either surname, so they reported
it to my grandma. Yeah! Such confusion and, while we were still on

    A Journey from Nowhere to Nowhere

that topic, I asked about the progress of the application with both departments that were involved and they told me that they had started receiving the grants in the previous months already.

"Owh! Well that's nice, I guess?" I enquired.

"Well, sisi, to be honest it is nice. At least this means that we will have money every month to use to buy the things that we need, plus some money gets to be saved every month," Zona explained

"Wow! It wasn't all bad, *mos* guys. I'm really happy for you guys. Now, you said something about some money being saved somewhere?" I probed further because I was curious.

Ande responded. "Eer Sisi, they told us that it is a condition from the social workers that some money, to the amount of R150, gets saved for each of us every month until we reach eighteen."

"That's awesome, guys. You see, really this didn't turn out all bad, nhe!"

Zona, smiling sheepishly, looked at me and said, "You know what, Sis'wam, if they had made me choose, I would choose to be happy, to be that person I was before this whole mess. I would still choose not to know my reality and have my peace."

Ande interjected. "Yah! Its true, *wena* sisi, what Zona is saying. But I am enjoying these trips to town and it looks like it's still going to be nice."

"Agh! Man, Mamgo," I said, "you know some things are bound to happen at some point. You were going to know your reality sooner or later. Let's just say that maybe this was not the most conventional way of finding out. Just take it one day at a time. So, what do you guys do in town? Must you be there all the time?"

"Oh yeah, sisi, we have to be there. We meet aunty in town, she gets the money, we go and buy groceries, we buy something to eat and she gives us some money to go shopping for clothes or whatever we want," confirmed Ande.

I tried to remember if these kids had ever been to town before this grant money came and I realised that they'd actually not been. I could remember a few times when I'd gone to town when I was growing up, but those occasions were because I had an ear infection and Mama was taking me to see the doctor in Tsolo. After some time there was a clinic in my village and there were no more trips to town; I had to walk that long distance from my home to the clinic in Ntywenka alone when the ear infection was back or, if I was very lucky, my friend Zozo would accompany me. So, the excitement that came with those trips to Tsolo was justifiable and understandable; I mean, I would have been ecstatic if it were me.

My granny was sleeping all the while we were having our night vigil, talking, singing and showing off some dance moves. Mamgo was a good dancer and she knew it. Mine was just to be a spectator. Shame, I was hopeless and I still am when it comes to dancing. All those dance moves (skere, Thobela and so on) looked easy, but I just couldn't do them. I could do traditional dance moves, though, and don't ask me what the difference is.

The truth is, even though I could see the pain in my siblings' eyes and hear the sadness in their voices, I felt like there was nothing I could do to make it better. I wanted to look for Jackie and Thembisa, but I had no clue where I would begin. Also, I was scared to even think of what it would do them if I tried and failed, or tried and didn't yield the desired results. I was not even sure what the desired results were at that stage, because it was difficult to gauge.

I promised myself that one day a chance would present itself for me to look for these two women and find them; they would have to come and account for their actions. They owed that to those poor kids and to my family too. That was a promise I made to myself, for them.

When I spoke to my grandma, she told me that the kids were not responding well to the change and she had had to talk to them about it from time to time. She honestly believed that, because they were still young – Zona entering her teens and Ande maybe around ten or eleven years old – they would heal and be able to move on. Her own words were, "Nothing has changed here at home towards them; we are still the same family, we are going to treat them the same way we have done over these years they have been here. Perhaps, when the cloud has cleared, they will be able to see that."

Now, as a grown up woman, I can see that nobody likes to formally address issues in my family; something will be said in passing or as if there's going to be another session where things will be discussed and put into perspective, but that never happens. I don't think there was a proper explanation to these kids as to what happened, when and how they ended up at our home with us and what had been done so far, as well as all the relevant information in terms of their history. The only version that they got was from the streets, and the bits and pieces I may have mentioned when I was confronted by Mamgo. I never told her the sequence of events because it was not my place; I was not told or given an instruction to do that.

As kids in those days, one couldn't question the elderly, the way children of these days do. I was a kid also and the thinking I have now as an adult is very different from the way I thought and saw things then. I therefore cannot blame anyone for the way things happened then and how they are nowadays. I somehow felt helpless in terms of what could be done to make the weight a bit lighter for them, but I didn't know anything about the existence of these people called psychologists or even about counselling, for that matter. I mean, we also had a lot of things to deal with as it was, even though our own parents had not abandoned us. I understand now that some things were too much for kids to have to bear, and some scars are only showing now that we are adults and we know only now that counselling is needed to deal with those issues that happened in our childhood. And all thanks to the changing times and education.

It's true when they say we deal with issues differently and that the outcome depends on how we deals with our issues. By the time these two hit their early teens they were already with my grandma on a full-time basis, as my mom had left for employment a few years back, leaving us with Granny, and after a while I also left for high school in Umtata. One of my three older brothers, Litha, was there and my father was also there, but they usually came home late at night from doing their jobs across the district and sometimes beyond. If they worked locally, it didn't make that much of a difference either, except for seeing them by chance if you were lucky. The arrangement had always been to cook and dish out my father's food and take it to his room, together with a jug of water for him to drink, and this was the same for my brother too. These people would leave very early in the morning and mostly we'd still be asleep, so I guess it wasn't really easy for them to notice anything untoward. As much as they were aware of the situation on the ground, I think there was nothing that anyone could do really, except hope that it would blow over and the kids would be fine again, if not fine already.

My grandmother was already in her eighties at the time I left home. By that time my younger brother was just a small boy, around ten or eleven, but he was already starting to misbehave, I guess reacting to this change that was brought upon them. They had also managed to get the foster care grant and now had access to money and, being aware that they had their own money, he would say that they could spend it anyhow, without anyone prescribing to them.

I observed this attitude on one or two occasions when it was that time of the month. Somehow I felt like there may be some over compensating going on, even though maybe it was not done

     A Journey from Nowhere to Nowhere

intentionally or consciously. Maybe it was jealousy talking, since I was in matric and flat broke all the time. My aunt would go to town with them to withdraw the money and buy some groceries for them and give them some money to buy things for themselves and I guess some had to be saved for them somewhere, as they had indicated to me. I noticed a change in their behaviour, especially from Ande, but at the same time I was just a child too. My granny was getting too old and was not so fresh and active anymore. I was going into my matric year and it was common knowledge that I would go to my mother in Cape Town after that. All my other siblings were living in Cape Town already, including Zitha, my younger sister. She had been schooling there for a few years

Indeed, the time came and I left home. Zona and I were still tight, but the relationship was not the same as it had been and to some extent I felt guilty for something that I didn't know. There was just this thing between us. We'd talk about this and that, only to find out that she somehow went back to square zero, where she had been before we talked. It was a constant battle she had with her emotions and the sense of betrayal, but I must say in all that she was still the sweetest baby sister I had. Such a warm-hearted, loving person and respectful to my grandma and elders, but also very stubborn.

ᴏᴏᴏᴏᴏ **Chapter 7** ᴏᴏᴏᴏᴏ

I LEFT FOR CAPE TOWN SO that I could either find a job or find a way to go to university. I did not have a phone where they could call me and neither did they. I watched our communication fade little by little until contact was lost completely. We didn't have means of keeping in touch. In fact, nobody had a cell phone at home at that time, including my mother. One would have to call the relatives just to find out if they had been seen at church on Sunday and that would be a consolation that they were okay.

Life was different in the township. There were public telephones where one could make a call for ninety cents per minute, but for me this was not of use as there was no phone at home to call. The plan of finding work proved to be difficult as I had just turned sixteen when I passed matric and everywhere I went to enquire for work they'd say I was still too young and should be at school. I hadn't got admission to university either, because I had not applied to any university, and that meant that I was to spend the whole year sitting at home doing nothing.

It was later in that year of sitting at home that one of my brothers, Thando, bought himself a second-hand NEC db2000 cellular phone, but later gave it to me to use. At least that was an assurance that once every month end I could get a call from home, but this was not to be. I communicated my number to Zona and asked her to call me when they got to town. There were those Vodacom containers with public phones in Tsolo as well, and we agreed. I guess that for them it was still not very easy to make phone calls, so we would chat very seldom. It was during those rare calls that I learned that Ande had dropped out of school or had been expelled on one or two occasions already.

"Ande is out of hand, sisi," a rather calm voice said on the other side of the phone. "He is seriously causing trouble wherever he goes, and sisi, he doesn't listen to Granny anymore – or anyone for that matter". That call must have been an SOS call by Zona, after feeling helpless and maybe hopeless in the situation that was playing itself out at home. But what could I do? When I asked to speak to him, she indicated that he had gone his own way after collecting the money from aunty, and she was all by herself at that moment.

This behaviour continued for some time and Zona would tell me, or rather update me, on everything, just like in the good old days. She came across as someone who had accepted herself and their situation, but the problems that plagued her younger brother had taken the centre of attention in her mind and she would cry when she told me what was going on there. On a few occasions I would speak to him, just to try and talk to him as his bigger sister, but after some time that didn't work. He would just be mad at Zona for telling me what he labelled as "lies" about him.

After some time, Zona managed to get a cell phone and I could call and talk to her and my granny. They were doing fine at home, under the circumstances. Grandma would also tell me about the challenges they were facing at home as the boy became naughtier by the day. In the village, my brother was becoming famous for mischief and this was embarrassing to the family. He would commit his atrocities even at home; even to the extreme of stealing some money

   A Journey from Nowhere to Nowhere

from my grandmother. All the good teachings and good upbringing was becoming a story, or something that seemed to have never existed in my brother's world. I don't even want to mention going to church, as that was where he was raised. Now, everything was just going very fast. The baby boy who was a few months old a few years back, the very handsome and sweet boy, disciplined and respectful, was nowhere. I remember we used to play together and sing together when we were growing up. The bright future that everybody in that yard had in their minds for him, the beautiful dreams that everybody had, was now doubtful.

I guess the normal thing to do to a naughty boy child back then would be to give him a hiding, just to bring him back on track, but believe me that trick was tried. My granny was not able to do that by herself anymore; I mean even when we were younger it was a job to give us a hiding. One of the brothers would have to hold us down or trap us and lock us inside the house as we would either run around the whole house, duck, dodge and hide under the table, under the bed, or literally hold the stick or her hands.

My father had to be the one to discipline Ande when he was back home. Ande knew that, due to our father's work schedule, it would take time before he could be apprised of his misdealings and he used that to his advantage. After a while, beating him didn't seem to be working anymore. He slept out on some nights without telling anybody, let alone getting permission. The suspicion of drug usage was not there yet. Even when Zona called when in town at month end and updated me on things at home, it never occurred to me that Ande could be using drugs. I guess that for us, coming from the rural areas, the issue of drugs was not well known at the time. It's difficult to say that the drugs were not there, but I think there was still very little information or awareness, if any at all, about drug availability and drug usage available to the villagers.

There were a number of instances where my grandmother's pension money disappeared without a trace and none besides him, Zona and Granny were staying in the house, and it was bad. He was said to have made bad friends with whom he spent the money. If he spent the money with them, on what remained a mystery.

After a while, it became clear that he was smoking something. Zona confronted him about it and, even though he never admitted to doing drugs, he never denied doing them either. He was spending a lot of his time in town and, when asked what he did there on a daily basis, he told Zona that she didn't understand. As time went by, incidents involving Ande in the neighbourhood also grew. There were suggestions that he and his friends could be getting cannabis in town because, when he was back, you could bet that he would eat and finish all the food inside the pot and eat the pot as well. He'd also be grumpy and dirty.

It became clear that whatever he was doing in Tsolo needed money. Granny had never lost money in the house before – not while our older brothers were there, not when we grew up and even with other cousins or boarders who lived there. Granny used to keep her money in the worst places one could ever imagine: match boxes, tied in a plastic bag, sometimes even in an old Aromat container and hidden somewhere, even in the garden on occasion. Whoever the culprit now was would find this money, take it and leave the container there. It became a strange, awkward and sad reality that someone would search for my granny's money and take it without permission. I felt terrible, as if I was there among the people who were suspects.

Ande would deny ever taking any money. I want to think that having access to money also contributed to some extent to the situation. I mean, since they'd started receiving the grant this boy had access to money and it was easy for him to go to town. He was broken, confused and had money at his disposal. Combine that with bad friends who could have been silly young boys as well, without a proper direction, and you have a problem. Maybe, when his money got finished, he would be desperate and that's when he would take my granny's money.

I realised from all that Zona told me that my little brother had come across the devil himself and there was the possibility of drugs, as tender as he was.

At some point he was trying to save himself from the mess and he started attending another local church, St. John's, where he was treated and guided. This move was greatly welcomed at home, even though the church he had gone to was not the church that he was raised up in with the family. This was good news after long years of trouble. My granny and the rest of the family had not stopped praying for him and we hoped for a renewal in his life. It is difficult not to have hope when you love a person. We had hope for change. We wanted change in his life. We loved him still, regardless.

Things seemed a bit better between the years 2004 and 2005, as he managed to start contact with me again. By that time I had a cell phone and I was a student at university as well. One morning I opened the door to my room coming from the shower, only to find my cell phone ringing… Eerr… "Who could it be early so?" I wondered, trying to see if I could recognise the number.

"Avoiding someone?" my roommate enquired.

"Ai, I don't know this number and I am not going to take it. I am late for my class as it is. They will call again some other time if they really want me." I tossed the cell phone on the bed and pulled my jeans from the cabinet. The bus to campus had been there for a while. Already the bus driver was revving, promising to leave anytime. It turned out later in that week that Ande was the one who called me on that particular morning.

Every once in a while, we would talk, but our talks were very brief because neither one of us had ninety cents to call the other every day. I would remind him about his dreams and encourage him to go back to school. One day, maybe after two whole years, he called me. He wanted to tell me about his excitement; that he had managed to get space at one of the local junior secondary schools where he was going to do his Standard 5, I think. By then he was already behind by three plus years, but it didn't matter. It was the best news he had told me in a while; being behind was nothing. I was super excited for him and just realised how much his nonsense was weighing on me and I thought that for my grandmother and his sister it was just unimaginable.

In the meantime, Zona had not done well at school a few times. She had failed a grade in one year and apparently had also not attended school well for another year due to ill health. That was a two-year setback for her, but I used to say to her that failing is not the end of the world. I had learned, almost too late in my life, that one can fail. When I attended university, that's when I learned that lesson. Even though I only found out two years later about her being sick and not being able to attend school at some point, it didn't matter anymore as she was healed from whatever had been making her sick. At least, that's what I was made to believe.

I sensed that our relationship was not as intact as it used to be anymore. If she could keep such information from me for that long, it meant that maybe she had someone else she was sharing these things with, or that she was secretive now. After I confronted her about it, she denied having replaced me and poured water over my own insecurities. Anyway, I let it go because she insisted that she was okay – 100%. By my own reckoning, she was supposed to have been starting Standard 8 at high school, but it turned out not to be – there was a delay. I had to postpone the excitement I had about her finishing school one day soon and going to university just like me although I was already picturing how things would be.

Anyway, the church that Ande had joined had other church branches, counterparts or other circuits in other local towns and surrounding areas. Like any other church, they would visit these circuits or branches to attend conferences or other church gatherings, as is a usual thing happening in all the churches. There was a time when my brother and other members from his church visited Reni, yes *the* Reni, where the same Thembisa who'd brought their mom to our home with small kids allegedly came from. I want to believe that for my brother this visit was rather more than just a church visit. Maybe this also brought some hope to him to find some answers. I mean, the information had already been out there as to what had happened some years ago. He was rather anxious and hopeful of finding "the Thembisa", or at least some information about her whereabouts.

Understandably, he did some research upon getting to Reni; asked around if people knew the surname of Thembisa. This is when he was directed to a home alleged to be her home, where he went and introduced himself. I want to believe that the people at that home received him just as my own family had done. They wouldn't really have known where he came from, except if he said he was a Rhadebe. Whatever my brother said to introduce himself to these strangers would determine whether he would get the information he was hoping to get about Thembisa and subsequently Jackie, his biological mother.

For some reason, I suspect that he must have said he was the son of Thembisa, or Zwelibanzi for that matter; that would only make sense. He must have thought of the possibility that these people might not know Jackie or that the two women had never gone there at all after leaving the children at my place. I mean, as much as my parents know a few of my friends, they don't know all the details about my friends. They know for sure my friends from my childhood, but they don't know the friends that I made upon arriving in Cape Town.

Now, going to a place where my mother was friends with a daughter there wouldn't necessarily yield the desired results, especially if the person didn't stay there anymore. One other reason that convinces me of this is the sudden interest shown by the folks there to meet his sister, Zona. I must say the guy may have felt some connection to the place and maybe the people there. What confuses me till today is whether this woman had passed on already when my brother went there, or was she still at large? Now, depending on what he said to them when he introduced himself, he might have got the information, but that he never shared. One other thing that convinces me that he had introduced himself as Thembisa or Zwelibanzi's son instead of Jackie's, is that he was determined to persuade his sister to go with him to Reni. There was even the idea of a ritual that would be performed for them by the people there. As far as I understand our customs, a family won't just perform a ritual for a stranger unless there is some form of blood relations.

There were subsequent visits to Reni undertaken by Andẹ in his own time and capacity, without going with the church. And I understand that there was no official or courtesy call or request to my family by this family about this boy's visit and their intentions towards the boy and his sister or to enquire about the children from my family. But having said that, I don't recall any communication between my family and this family even back then, when their son Zwelibanzi was being raised at my home. The only person who is said to have been brought by the brother after some time is this Thembisa woman.

The idea of Zona going with Ande to Reni was not well received by her. Unfortunately, she never hid her own feelings about the so-called newly-found family that wanted to see her. Her view was always about the way these people wanted to do things. She often questioned why they didn't make time to come to our home to meet them, now that they had discovered that there were people like them and, I won't lie, I supported her there. She declined completely to go and see them.

Chapter 8

LIFE HAS ITS OWN WAY of how things go, and I lost contact with Zona, again. I was drawn to other things that were happening in my life as a young woman; having a child before completing university, dropping out of university, finding a job and a whole lot of other things – the good and bad that come with all that. In year 2006, during the June holidays, I was already working but my employment contract was coming to an end and I took the opportunity to visit home for a few days with my daughter and we had a great time.

The visit was very important to me. I wanted to see my granny and I wanted to see my siblings and my other family members; it had been a while since I'd left home. Everyone seemed in good health, overjoyed to have me back, even if it were just for a few days. The kids seemed to have accepted their status quo. In our talks about the future, the issue about the surname came up again. Zona said she was worried that her matric certificate would have that surname and that she didn't understand why all of a sudden this surname mattered. She said that at times she felt betrayed and not protected by our family from being bullied by social services just because they needed the foster care money, but she understood that my granny was old and Mom didn't really have much and they were growing and had needs.

I asked her what she would have preferred if she had been given the chance to make a decision about the issue and she said, "Sisi, we have been here at home for almost fifteen years now, if not more, and before this issue of money came about I was almost thirteen years old. We grew up with this home full of people, including you, sisi, and our other siblings. It was tough, but we made it. Why now is the issue of money so important that it turns our world upside down? As if the fact that our mother had abandoned us is not big enough, sisi? Now, to be expected to use the surname of someone who hated us so much as to come all the way from Jozi to abandon us with people she never knew before? How does that become fair, sis' wam?"

I sat there staring and listening to her, thinking. Then I replied and said, "You know what, Mamgo *mntase,* that sucks! It really sucks and I think you are right." What else could I say to my girl? My God, I felt that she was absolutely correct and if I were in her shoes I would feel exactly like that, period. There was no doubt about that. "And you know what else, *mntase?*" I asked. "From my own perspective it doesn't matter what surname one uses because the surname doesn't make a person. It's just a way of being identified."

I even made examples of people who choose to take their clan names as surnames instead. Obviously, this justification of mine was hitting a brick wall. I was not making sense, was I? I said, "You know what, Mamgo? Believe it or not, we love you and Sgwili, unconditionally so. My family would never go out of their way to hurt and destroy you now, after sticking with you when you were brought here as a three-year-old and Ande just a few months old. I'm sure this went to a stage where no one knew it would. No one here at home would want you guys to be called by some strange identity after investing so much in you guys, emotionally and financially. This application for a foster care grant was made with good intentions for you and your brother, and not to hurt you. I end here. To us, or let me speak for myself, you will always be that Mamgo that I love, regardless of the surname on your official documents."

At least I saw a smile in that teary face of hers and she said, "Promise?"

"I promise you, *mntase*." I assured her that I would always be there, regardless of what happened.

"Okay, ke Sisi wam, I'm happy."

I must say that she looked thin – not that she had ever been fat at any time in her life, but she'd had a normal body weight that was acceptable – and now her face was just rough, full of acne, probably because of the stage she was at, I guess, and because she'd had no real guidance in terms of what sort of facial products to stay away from and which ones to try. Remember that this person had money to buy cosmetics every month all by herself, and I know, when I was a teen myself, I used to take my mom's snow white facial cream and use it without her permission. I still get embarrassed and can't believe some of the things I bought to use on my face when I got to varsity; the face that didn't have any need for such things. Imagine what a thirteen or a fifteen year old would buy.

We had brief talks with the Ande. He would disappear early in the morning and come back late, but generally he was okay. He was trying hard to stop being naughty. He didn't bother my granny anymore and he was trying to be a good boy who could be trusted again by his family, but I think he was still facing a huge battle with completely stopping. One could not say that he had stopped smoking whatever he used to smoke, but generally his behaviour had improved. He would go out during the day and come back home late in the evenings, but after all he was a boy and boys go to playing fields and maybe to other villages to attend *imigidi* or weddings or whatever occasion. We couldn't expect this boy to be sitting with women in the house the whole time. I mean, that was too much to ask, or was it? While I was home, when he came back in the evenings we would chat briefly and he'd play with my daughter. He loved kids and kids loved him.

Soon, my few days were over and I had to go back to Cape Town to find out if my employer would extend my employment as they had not indicated anything yet. I used to work in a company where I was an admin assistant/ tea girl / receptionist / secretary. As much as they had not said anything with regard to the extension of my contract, I was confident that they needed me there. They would not easily find a graduate who would settle for all those demands for one thousand Rand fortnightly. I was a bargain, if you know what I mean.

Everybody continued with their lives as usual. Zona and Ande were already teenagers and seemed to have calmed down and were taking care of my grandmother. We'd have our random chats whenever she called. I think there were public phones, at least in the village, where one could make a call. But I still had to rely on her calling as I could not call her back because they did not have a phone at home anymore as something had happened to Zona's cell phone

I can't think of any reason why she wasn't bothered by the fact that she didn't have a cell phone, besides that maybe cell phones where still regarded as older people's things, or working people's things, and maybe it was still uncommon for a learner to own a cell phone then.

There was a time when my brother was accused of having stolen some money from the neighbour's house. This allegation came about at the time when my brother was out and about and was known to have a reputation for being naughty. Much as my family was trying very hard, it was still difficult to trust him completely with anything. He had told too many lies and had done too much, even at home. Even though he denied it, it was difficult to believe what had really happened, as it was alleged that he had been sent to the house by the owner to get something for her and he went to the house as he was requested, but after that the money that was kept in the house was missing. You can imagine the awkwardness of the situation when he denied it all, the embarrassment that my grandmother and Zona must have felt. They did not know what to believe because Ande had been trying to convince them that he had changed.

At first I was mad because I'd experienced situations where people take advantage of you because you are poor, or they undermine you because you are lower than them. Situations where they'll use you and, after using you, instead of saying thank you, they spit in your face and accuse you of stealing their belongings just for the fun of it. I bet I must have been under my brother's spell already by then. I believed him when he said he wanted a new leaf in his life. My first reaction was, "Why would she send him to her house knowing that he is a thief and not send her own son?"

At the same time I was angered by my brother's version of events, which was full of contradictions, and also traumatised by the threats that came with all that drama. I remember that Zitha went mad when she heard about the accusations that were levelled against Ande; as if she had read my mind or she was there when I asked why the woman had sent Ande to her house knowing very well that he was a thief and that she had money in the house. Zitha's exact words were "She was setting him up, *mos*! You can't put a goat in your vegetable garden and think that it's going to sleep there and not eat your cabbages. She's mad."

There were curses that were thrown left, right and centre at whoever had stolen the money. I wondered how much this money was, but I never got to know the amount. What I know is that whoever had taken that money was going to continue taking people's things until he or she met his or her mates; people who would be equal to his mischiefs and teach him a lesson. If I'd had my way, I would have paid that money back, because sometimes you just have to be scared because a tongue is a very powerful weapon. If a person cursed you back then, even if you knew that you didn't do what they believed you did, or even if you did it, you'd better apologise while you still had time.

All I can say is that I deduced from the stories that my brother told regarding the issue of the money that went missing that he was not honest about the issue. He might have not been the one who took the money, but he knew who had taken it and he would downplay the curses and threats and chuckle and say, "Sisi, people are going to be surprised, I tell you. They will be surprised and they will cry".

I was tired of all these mind games and whatever it was that he meant. I was not there with him when he was sent to the house, and he definitely didn't share the money with me. If he had stolen it, he must have spent it with his friends. You get confused when you have a thief in the house. The dilemma was that he was on his way to recovery, attending church, had stopped stealing granny's money, was attending school again and I think that's what made things even more confusing for us. You can trust me about the kind of manipulation that these guys have up their sleeves in situations like that, almost as if you had asked them to steal or be bad people in the first place. You can't raise your eyes without them playing that guilt trick card on you, as if you don't believe they could change and be better people.

Anyway, we had our talks here and there with my brother regarding his time to go to the mountain and all that comes with that; I mean, he was grown. In my tradition it is a norm that when a boy becomes a man there will be celebrations in the family and the villagers also join in in the celebration. This celebration is called *umgidi*. It is done to welcome back home a boy who has gone to the mountain and comes back home as a man. It comes with a lot of expenses, as a cow has to be slaughtered, a goat has to be slaughtered, and sometimes even one or two sheep, plus there's food, gifts, drinks

     A Journey from Nowhere to Nowhere

(alcohol), depending on the number of people and visitors that one is expecting. And it is expected that new clothes be bought for the new man. During our discussions about this, I'd encourage my brother to concentrate on his schooling while we tried to gather some money together so that we could do *umgidi* for him. I encouraged him not to succumb to the pressure that his age mates and friends were leaving him behind. He would hear what I was saying, but I could tell that he was not convinced or that he didn't understand well, as he usually said in a soft voice, "I hear you, Sisi".

It was not long after that a call from home came to inform us that my younger brother had gone to the mountain, and that he had done so without anyone knowing about it. Under normal circumstances, a boy would be taken by his father or uncle or any older person delegated by the family to accompany the boy to the initiation school, and then from there a place would be prepared for him far away from the community, preferably in the mountains or bush where there were no regular visitors, as this is considered very sacred and secretive. Women are not allowed to go anywhere near the place, apart from the young girls who would be preparing the food for the boys.

In my brother's situation, this was not the case. My father had not okayed him to go and had not prepared or arranged for someone or taken him. I was disappointed, of course, and I didn't know what to say. I kept on wondering, "Why can't this person toe the line for once, for heaven's sake?" I learned that actually with him it doesn't matter what one says; Ande does what he decides to do anyway. Now I was challenged to either give up on him or continue offering him advice, even though I knew that he didn't care.

This reminded me of what my granny used to say about Ande. She used to look at him and say, "This is another kind. Pity we don't know what kind". She would say this when she was exhausted by the troubles that Ande caused, even as a small boy. My mother repeated the same exact words of Granny at some point, also tired from all the never-ending drama around Ande.

Nobody had money saved somewhere – basically, there was no money – and I had told him that and we had agreed on a specific timing, but nonetheless he had gone against all that. My older brothers handled it the way men do, but it was done and I heard them saying, "It's fine. What's done is done," and they were excited to welcome the boy back.

My grandmother was disappointed and a bit hurt by the whole thing. I guess it was also because of being anxious and not knowing what to expect as a mother. Too many boys don't make it back for one reason or the other. Now, every day we found ourselves praying a never-ending prayer until we knew that he was okay and would be coming back home in a matter of few weeks.

Then he was back and everybody forgot the stress and disappointment we'd gone through as a result of his actions. We were just happy to have him back alive and healthy and being a new man now. I'm almost sure it was everybody's prayer that from that moment he would shun his funny tricks and do what grown man do. There's this notion that being naughty is associated with being an old boy, and I don't know where it came from, but you'd often hear the elderly saying that it's being an old boy that's causing a person to do funny things and that once a person becomes a man all those old silly things pass away. This was my prayer for Ande and my granny was happy and hoped that great things would follow for my brother.

ᵒᵒᵒᵒᵒ **Chapter 9** ᵒᵒᵒᵒᵒ

A YEAR LATER, MY SISTER ZITHA went to visit them at home during the December holidays and they were partying together over the festive season. This was great, they were happy and healthy and finally the girls had cell phones now again so one could call and also they could call. A few months down the line, my family back at home was preparing for my *lobola* negotiations and Zona and Ande were part of that. Zona played a big role as a young sister who was available there at the event.

In my culture, as umXhosa, the in-laws coming to ask for a hand in marriage will bring all sorts of gifts to the family of the intended bride, or they will be asked for all sorts of funny, sometimes ridiculous, gifts by the family they are marrying into; things like sweets for the girls (daughters) in the house. Gifts could be in a form of money, drinks or even the real sweets. Mamgo was there and she sure maximised her chances of scoring some sweets. She was very excited as she told me how much fun she'd had; it was almost as if she were the one getting married.

I think that after this period we lost communication for a period as long as a year or so, as my own life took a certain turn. This time I was at fault because I just isolated myself from everyone. I had my fair share of depression. I was consumed too much by my own troubles, to the extent that I lost track of time and I lost connection with a lot of the people whom I loved.

The whole of year 2008 was a year of trouble for me; far from what it had promised to be when it began on the 1ˢᵗ of January. By the time things were starting to normalise in my life, I learned that Mamgo had been sick for some time. If I remember correctly, it must have been early in the year 2009 when I learnt about that, but by that time she was no longer sick, or at least that is what I was made to believe. Also, Ande was still back at school and my grandma was happy.

I was happy to hear the good news, but I had noted the secrecy around Zona's sickness with concern. Her having been sick was a surprise, because she hadn't told me for the second time around. I wondered about it, but dismissed it as maybe something that was not serious and that she didn't want to bother me about and, moreover, I was the one who had gone AWOL for some time. Nonetheless, I did not remember telling people not to call me and there was never a time when I didn't take the calls from my family; I just didn't call them and kept to myself. Maybe Zona was going through a phase similar to mine, and those who got to know about her being sick were privileged because they were there at home with her. "Anyway, my brothers would have told me if it was something big." I tried to convince myself with these kind of reasoning.

After calling her a number of times and not succeeding in getting through, I remember getting home from work and telling my mother about it and she said she had heard the other time that she was not well and wondered if it was the same pain that was said to be in her back.

"*Hayibo*! Mama! So I was the only one who didn't know about it?" I asked my mom.

"*Wethu*! It didn't sound to be something serious, and by the time I heard it was something of the past," she said.

"I just wonder why Zona doesn't say when she's not well. Really, I don't get it."

"You know what, my child, I'm thinking. If this pain in her back does not go away completely, maybe during the June school holidays she should come and visit us here in Cape Town, so we could take her to some doctors or even hospitals with better facilities, to see if they could maybe see something. What do you think?"

"Oh yes, Mama, I think that is a great idea too. What did you say was wrong with her again, Mah?"

"Well, I'm not so sure, but it had something to do with a back pain," she explained.

"Awu! Why would Zona have a back pain, na?" I exclaimed. "She's a baby *mos* herself, and since when do babies get to have back issues such that people will say that you have been sick?"

"Hey, Zowi, I wonder also," my mother said.

We agreed that I would speak to my grandma and hear her own views about it. We wanted Zona to come to Cape Town for the holidays, hoping to be able to get her x-rays or have some tests done on her in the hope of finding out what could be wrong with her back. And since she had always been a sickly person, we wanted proper check-ups done on her. We believed that at least that would not be as difficult to do in the city as compared to the villages. The hospital facilities are way better in the big cities when compared to the rural areas, and access to those facilities is also much easier in the big cities than back at home. I was sure my granny would welcome the idea with both hands.

I was as excited about her visit as if it were finalised already. I knew that it was a matter of one year before she finished school and soon she would have to make a choice of which university to go to to further her studies, and I was hoping that she would say Cape Town. In my mind, everything was calculated. I had been trying to convince my granny to come and visit us and probably this would be the best timing. She could come with my sister and then, boom! We'd be able to kill two birds with one stone.

You know, sometimes one just wishes one could just hold the hands of time and not let go of the good times. I was just missing my family, with all the noise we used to make, and reminiscing about all the precious times we used to have, times that one doesn't have any more just because of time and, of course, because of growing up.

I was already busy trying to play the detective role on the side, even though only my best friend knew about it. I had not told anyone about it at home. I was wiser and curious and also trying to find answers for my siblings. I had acquired a lot of knowledge about doing research on the internet and knew which departments to approach. I had a few contacts in places that could help trace the two women who had left these siblings of mine behind.

It was that same deadly May that I encountered my first dead end. My only possible link was no more. She had passed on a few years ago already. Yes, you heard right! The same Thembisa who'd brought Jackie, the mother of Zona and Ande, was no more. After visiting the Department of Home Affairs' website, I browsed anxiously through for the self-help service to verify the status of three people. I wanted to check Thembisa, Jackie and Zwelibanzi. Sometimes at home they thought that maybe these children were fathered by Zwelibanzi, hence the sister Thembisa brought them to our place where her brother had once stayed and grew up.

The search for Zwelibanzi Mnyani didn't yield any results. "Dammit! Does this mean that the bastard doesn't exist?" I asked that computer, but there was no response. "Come on now, maybe I fed in the incorrect spelling... Eerr... le... t-t m –e see. Nothing is incorrect *mos* here. Mfxm! Go to hell.

"Let us check Jackie and see what we'll get... J-a-c-k-i-e Mdledle..." and nothing. Okay, let's spell it another way... J-a-c-k-e-y Mdledle" and still nothing. I could have lifted that computer and thrown it on the floor if it were mine, but I had to respect other peoples' property. But Jackie is the name on those clinic cards, *mos*? I slid my fingers through my hair. "Could these three bastards be fake people? How is it possible? Am I doing something wrong in my search? It can't be! It's clear *mos* that these people are using different names, wherever they are. They have duped my family by using fake names. Yerr!"

When I searched for Thembisa Mnyani, I stared at that computer screen in disbelief. I could feel tears starting to well up in my eyes. She was dead. "Wow! This is something! Really?" I spoke those words softly with disbelief, mostly doubting the information. I don't know why this result didn't cause me to swear or curse just the way I did with the first two results. I guess it must have been respect for the dead, maybe? Who knows? All I know is that the result for Thembisa pierced my chest through to my heart. I could feel my heart starting to race very fast, accompanied by terrible stomach cramps. I had to sit backwards on my chair and try to calm myself down. A quick thought came to mind, and I remembered that I needed to check more or less the age of the deceased Thembisa to see if it was close to one I was looking for, before crying for nothing. Tears were flowing from my eyes and I could barely see. It somehow felt worse than not finding anything out about them.

I was disappointed. I had to swallow the lump in my throat and move on. At least it was better because I was the only one who knew about it. I knew that I would tell Zona when she visited during June holidays about whatever information I might have that could lead us to these people and, to be honest, I was optimistic about it. I was hoping for good news. I believed that deep down it would give them closure. But the reality that I was faced with, I couldn't tell her. It was nothing close to what I had hoped for: finding these people having fun somewhere and getting them to explain themselves and their cruel actions.

The day that I was sad and down from hitting a brick wall happened to be Mother's Day. There she calls, with her soothing voice. "Hi, sis wam!" she said. "Yhoooo, I know that you have been calling me and I got your messages. I'm so sorry, man, you know these phones are not reliable sometimes. You know I love you, *mos*, sisi *wam andithi?*" There was always that demanding sense of ownership that wouldn't allow you not to forgive her.

We laughed about it and I asked her, "Wena! What's this I'm hearing about you not being well again? What's up? And why didn't you tell me about it? Since when do we keep things from each other now?"

She laughed out loud and said, "No man, sisi. I had this pain in my back but now it's gone. I'm fine, sisi, believe me. I went to the clinic and was given pain tablets and they really helped me." Anyway she was calling because she was looking for Mama. "Where's Mama? I'm looking for her," she says. "I was calling her phone but I'm not winning – is she around? I wanted to wish her a happy Mother's Day and I missed her today."

Luckily for her I was home already from work and Mama was also at home that afternoon. "Wait a little – let me get her on the phone. Mama, Zona is on the line for you," I said, passing the phone over to Mom. They had a nice chat and laughed about the things they were talking about. I heard Mama telling her about what we had discussed about her coming during the June school holidays so that she may be seen by the doctors that side and that was okay.

     A JOURNEY FROM NOWHERE TO NOWHERE

She was excited and the only thing left was for me to speak to my grandma about it.

It was hardly two weeks later, and I was at work. Just before lunch my phone vibrated… "Brrr, brrr, brrr" Oh! It was my brother Vusi.

"Hello, Rhadebe!" I answered with excitement.

"Hey, sisi, are you at work? Can we talk?"

"Yes, *bhuti*, I am at work, but yeah, we can talk. What's up?"

"Hey, *mntase*, I just received some disturbing news, man. This girl Mamgo has left us. She passed on in the early hours of this morning, they say." I was just listening on the other side. "Sisi, are you still there?" he called.

"Oh yeah… yeah, I am *bhuti*, I'm… I'm still here …" I said.

"Okay, Rhadebe, I'm just calling with the bad news, man, and I'm… Yeah, it's like that, my sister," he mumbled.

"Wow! It's okay *bhuti*. Thanks," was all I said to my brother. That was a very bad phone call for the day.

"Ah! Dammit, Zona!" I blurted out. I stood there for a minute, clutching my cell phone and thinking about what my brother had said to me. For a moment I was convinced that I was losing it. I doubted if I had received the phone call at all. This thing was affecting me so that I believed I was seeing things and getting calls when I had not. "Did he just say she…? No, man! I don't think I heard correctly. It's not possible, man… Let me just call him again and find out what he was saying to me, or if he really called me at all." By this time I was beginning to shake and my phone just slipped through my hands and fell to the floor.

"Is everything alright, Zowi?" asked one of my colleagues. "You seem upset? Did something happen?"

"Eish! One of my brothers just called me to tell me that this young girl is gone… like gone! Dead, in other words," I responded.

"What girl are you talking about, wena Zowi?" exclaimed another colleague from the other side of the room. At that moment I just stood up and left for the bathroom. I could feel that my chest was just closing in. I needed some air and some calm. Didn't need no questions.

"She's no more… hehe! This must be some sick joke, nhe!" I sat down in the bathroom for a while. "Okay Zowi, call Vusi! That's the only way to find out what he was saying."

"You have insufficient airtime to make a call. Please load air…."

"Shut up! Nx! Who asked you? What the hell is this? I don't have airtime?" *Okay, dear. Calm down! You are most probably panicking for nothing here.* There was that resounding voice that whispered within me. *"She's fine, she's not dead."* I left the bathroom and went back to the open plan office. I called her phone right away, now using the landline on my desk, but it went to voice mail.

"Hi, this is Zona. You know what to do."

It was all a lie. I told myself that there was no such a thing as Zona's passing. "She can't die now, *mos*! She's too young. What could have happened?" This left the sound of a siren in my ears. I couldn't hear anything for a while, like the lights had just gone off or there was load shedding. Could it be the same story of a pain on her back, maybe? Nah, man, it can't be. She'd just told me last week that she was okay and the pain was gone.

I had to make a few phone calls to the people back home to find out what was really happening. Apparently, the same pain in her back had attacked her when she was attending some sports activities at one of the local high schools in the community. She had left her friends there, saying that she was feeling cold and had back pain again and that she was going home to sleep. My brother Litha heard about it and when he got home she was in a bad state. He carried her, because she couldn't walk by herself anymore, and they managed to take her to the hospital in Tsolo, where she was attended to. When he left she was under the care of the doctors.

That was the crazy story told to me. It sounded unreal, and I mean, seriously, she can't do that, *mos*. Tried calling her phone a few more times and the same voice mail message answered.

"Dammit, Zona! Why are you doing this, man, yhe? Why are you doing this?" I asked. I left my desk again and this time even went completely outside the office to get some air. I completely broke down this time around. It hurt – a whole lot. I couldn't believe it, but it hurt so badly. I couldn't help but feel this tightness in my chest, like I was struggling to breathe, and I had to keep my hands on my chest. There was a sharp pain or heaviness that felt like it was pulling me to the ground. I took note of the sensation and, as I bent there, leaning against the stair rail, I realised that it was actually not the first time I'd felt that sensation. I knew the feeling was familiar; when something is really heavy for me to handle emotionally, I get that feeling and it becomes extremely difficult to recover. It used to get so intense that it'd get me worried that one day I might not make it. Now, when I felt that pain I knew it was the beginning of a very hectic period for me. For the larger part of my life I've struggled with expressing myself, especially grief. I had to sit there and make a conscious decision. I knew that I had to live for my two small kids so I had to cut through this feeling of sorrow and grief that had struck me. I had to find a way around it.

"Okay, what now, Lord?" I asked. "Seriously?" I asked again. "I mean, just like that, Lord? You allowed her to die?" One minute I was praying and the next minute I was denying whatever I had heard about the death of my younger sister. I sat there in that basement trying to think.

"*Nha, man! The news can't be true, but if it is true, it is okay, I guess. I will see everything when I get home. It means that I need to go home soon.*"

And I shelved it. Yes! Just like that! I forgot about it intentionally because it didn't make sense to me. Imagine, on top of my tight chest I still had to be squeezed more in the train on my way to Maitland train station. I needed all the strength to board and exit the train, otherwise I wasn't going to make it. I think that was the moment I tried to learn to "shelve" things early, rather than prolonging them, in order to control my anxiety attacks. I was also afraid of dying and leave my children without a mother. I told myself that I was going to wait for month end, which was just a few days away, and then I would go home. Everything else would be clear when I got there. Maybe it was because I hadn't been home for a while and this was just a trick to get me home.

After work I went home to meet my mother and Zitha. I guess people were just numb. There was nothing much discussed about the issue at hand. Each one was just trying to be busy with something. Mama just took the dirty clothes outside and started ferrying water from the tap and there she was, washing the clothes. Zitha's face was full of disappointment, but she's not a talker and after a while, after having been focused on her cell phone, she just stood up and started cooking.

I asked if she thought we'd be able to go home together for the funeral and she didn't even look at me. She shrugged her shoulders and answered me in a low voice that she didn't know. After a few days, a date for the funeral was communicated from back home. In the meanwhile I called nobody there. The only phone number I kept on dialling on a daily basis was Zona's. Even at night I would try her phone, over and over. Day in, day out, I called her cell phone number a number of times. The phone didn't ring, but it would go to voice mail. "Hi, this is Zona. You know what to do." I would listen to her voice message command, over and over.

Death is so unfair. It is so permanent, and it doesn't give you a chance to say that one more thing you would like to tell the person you love. Once it has struck, it doesn't matter whether it was just a minute ago that you saw the person, the person won't hear you and won't answer back. If only I could be given that one minute to say something to her before she died.

"Ayh, Zowi. She has decided to hide away and depart from you without saying anything. Maybe she didn't want you to say anything to her. Just forget about her. She betrayed you, not once and not twice. This child was sick a few times and she did not tell you. Now think about that as her 'best' sister. Maybe you were not her closest person, as you want to believe. And, besides, this is not your mother's child. She's not your real sister. Maybe you should start treating her that way. She has done just that to you, *mos*." Those were the words of my husband. I could see that he found it difficult to understand why I was down and upset by the issue of Zona's passing.

"Wena! You don't understand, and you will never understand. If you don't have anything sensible to say about this, please do me a favour and stay out of it. I don't need your nasty and uncultured comments," I responded harshly.

"Hayke! Suit yourself, madam. I was just pointing out the obvious," he said, while making an exit from the kitchen, leaving me raging alone there.

"How could you say that? You should be ashamed of yourself! Nx!" I still followed him with those sharp words. But, in all honesty I did feel betrayed and all the things he said seemed true, and maybe too true.

The day came for us to leave for the Eastern Cape. My mom and I braced ourselves as we took a bus that would travel overnight, and I can still remember that I had a small baby at the time. My son was only seven months old. On the way I was facing the crisis of being in denial of the reason why I was heading home, and lying to myself that everything would be fine; that I would see this girl when I got home. Part of me was trying to deal with the sense of betrayal that I felt. Maybe my husband was right. Part of me felt like I deserved better treatment from her, but then again I cautioned myself against the thought of her death. I mean, I wanted her not to be dead so much.

My mom and I did not talk much about it either, although the one thing I remember my mom saying regarding Zona's death was, "*Bayayenza into man ababantwana yhuu!*" meaning that their drama was just too much.

⬦⬦⬦ **Chapter 10** ⬦⬦⬦

THE FOLLOWING DAY WE GOT to Umtata, in a taxi to Tsolo and then another taxi to my village, eNgcele. After almost an hour I heard Mama telling the driver that we were about to get off at Adonis bus stop.

"Alright," said the driver and, after a few minutes shouted, "There you are Mama. Adonis stop." We got off with our bags and I put the baby on my back and we headed for home. My village looked exposed and barren from lack of vegetation and maybe because of the cold weather, as it was in winter. The grass and everything else looked brown, dull and with no sense of life whatsoever. When I looked around, all I saw was hopelessness.

The bus stop is uphill and you see my home from an elevated view. All I was interested in was whether I would see a lot of people, or some movement at home. I could hear my heart beat. It was like it would rip my chest open. My hands were sweating. All of a sudden I was enveloped by nerves. I can't say I had really experienced a loss so close to me before. I was afraid that if it were true that my sister was no more, I was not ready for that and therefore didn't know how it would affect me. I was also afraid on my granny's part; I wasn't sure how that would affect her. Zona had been her pillar of strength since

I'd left home for the city. My mother was showing a strong character so I wasn't really much concerned about her. Plus, she still had me and Zitha.

I kept my fingers crossed and my thoughts were completely taken over. *"Nha, it's nothing man. Get home and Makhulu is going to tell you the truth about what's happening here,"* I convinced myself. Walking down the hill, Mom was just quiet. I guess I had also been quiet for some time and maybe she was in her own meeting, just like I was.

"I don't see a lot of people there, Mama. It's like there's no one at home," I commented. All I wanted was an assurance from her that everything looked okay and that we were being pranked.

"I'm sure there are people, my girl, maybe just not outside." There goes my hope for an assurance; through the window. "It's going to be okay, my child. This shall pass. Just allow yourself to go through it," she said. It was like my mother could read my mind.

In a matter of minutes we arrived at home and greeted some people who were seated outside in front of the house. It was not possible to see them as we came from behind the houses, from the bus stop. I quickly searched their eyes, hoping to find something that would confirm or deny if there really was death at home. I found nothing in their eyes, intentionally so. I followed my mother as we went inside my granny's house. My aunts were there with my granny and, as we were shaking hands with everyone in the house, I was just scanning the house to search for the mood and I didn't pick up anything untoward. Anyway, one person in the house started a song and we prayed.

"Yha nhe!" I sighed.

After praying, my granny started to speak, addressing my mom and I. "*Wena* Nobahle and Zowi, my child's child. This young girl Zona has departed from this earth as you must have heard. She was not well. She had this pain on her back that she always complained

        A JOURNEY FROM NOWHERE TO NOWHERE

about. She had been to the clinic and they gave her some pain medication but after some time the pain came back again and she would always sleep. It is clear to see that last week it became too strong for her and finally took her away. And that's how she died."

Some people in the house were busy making sounds and nodding their heads in agreement with what my grandmother was saying. I felt like screaming and saying, "Shut up and stop nodding your heads," because I didn't need their agreement. Whether they nodded their heads or not, it was not going to change the situation and that was what I wanted: a different situation where my sister would be alive. I wanted the situation to be changed, not confirmation from them.

"Wow! Okay, what did the doctors say it was, *Makhulu*?" my mother enquired.

"I don't really know, sisi, you must speak to Litha. He'll know these things, and he was there with her," she said.

You know when they say it doesn't rain but it pours? That was how I was feeling. Life was a bit rough for me and a lot of things were going on in my personal space and, like my sister, no one knew what I was going through and I was in pain alone and at the same time had responsibilities at home and at work. People start telling you that you know God was there when it happened, how you must not question God for this, how you must release the person and let the person rest, how you must not cry as if you doubted God and as if you are not a believer.

I won't lie; this whole thing was somehow not real, in the sense that I was expecting my younger sister to enter the house and negate this idea of her being dead. Apparently, my brother had gone to town to transfer her to another mortuary. That was the response I got when I was looking for him to confirm and get more details. When the sun set without Zona entering the house, as I had been hoping, I started getting myself involved in preparations of whatever was going on.

The second morning came and she was not there. I told myself that maybe if I could see the body I would believe that she was no more. Luckily enough, the day after that my aunts would go to the mortuary to dress her in preparation for the funeral, so I asked if I could go with them and my mother encouraged me to go.

In the meantime, while we were going to the mortuary some family members went to attend her memorial service at the school where she was doing Grade 10 or 11. We went to Maclear, bought some clothes and headed for the mortuary, but when we got there it was for some reason not possible to dress her and we were asked to leave the clothes and told that she would be prepared by the staff there. Okay, that was difficult for me to understand; I mean we left the house going to the morgue to dress Zona and that didn't happen. And I couldn't hear the real reasons. Much as I was freaked out to be at the mortuary I still wanted to see my sister – for my own sanity.

Anyway, I didn't question anything because my aunts seemed to understand what was being said by the person who attended to us. Everything he said kept going past me – maybe being in the mortuary had closed my ears, like literally. A mortuary is a creepy place, even if one is just in the reception area. I guess those crazy stories of ghosts and people waking up in the mortuary while being bathed had a contribution to my sudden deafness.

We left the mortuary and faced home again. I must say, I have the craziest aunts in this world. In fact, my whole family is crazy, even my uncles are very funny. So this trip both to and from Maclear was just on another level. Listening to these two aunts of mine going on and on about their own things just managed to crack a smile on my face and eventually laughter, and I forgot about Zona and her death for a while. We got home and joined other family members who were making arrangements for a night vigil for Zona. I had to attend to my baby also and, before I knew it, it was already time for the night vigil to begin.

In the process, I also gathered that the so-called foster care grant money had stopped a while ago. Apparently, they were older than the qualifying age now, though I didn't probe much about that. I kept on going back and forth, asking myself if all the stress, trouble, emotional turmoil that these two kids were put thorough was all for a mere few years? If it was all worth it? Really? I could not help wondering if this stress didn't have something to do with my sister's untimely death. Anyway, I never spoke to anyone about it because I just wanted to pass through the emotional turmoil I had as a result of her death.

Sometimes, I would try and call her phone number still. I don't know whether I was hoping she'd answer or it was more of wanting to hear her voice mail. You know, when people closest to you regard you as a strong person, you are actually at a disadvantage because you have to keep strong and keep the brave face, even when you are actually falling apart. That is the story of my life. I had to try and continue with my life as if I hadn't lost a sister; a person who had invaded my childhood from nowhere and became a huge part of it. Some people, like my younger brother Ande and some of my colleagues, were not expecting the impact that losing my younger sister had on me as "she was not my mom's child". Even my own husband didn't take this loss seriously. To some, it was just one of those things that has happened. I had to be okay quickly, as according to them it was not a real loss of a sibling.

On the night of the vigil I got a chance to speak to my younger brother about what was happening and he didn't really have much to say – just like me, maybe.

What he told me was, "You know, sisi, I spent a lot of time messing around, doing things that hurt my family and embarrassed my family and my sister. Now, when I was trying to make up for that, she decides to leave, sisi. Do you know what this means for me sis' wam? That I'm all alone in this life. I know and understand that you guys are here for me as my family, but this means that the only true sibling that I had in this life has decided to leave me alone in this world, just like our mother did.

"And you know what else, sis' wam? It means that I never took care of my sister. I was supposed to be there for her, to know if she was not well, and maybe we could have got her all the help she needed in time." We were sitting behind the house the night of her night vigil and the tears were just running down our faces. I was overwhelmed by the whole thing: the tears, the sorrow that displayed in my brother's face and his voice. I was trying to think how my granny must be feeling and that would fill my heart with sorrow. Generally, it's difficult to read how my granny and my mother are feeling because they just don't express their feelings. It felt like their own sorrow was more justified than mine. All the drama leading to Zona's death, her secrecy, the nonsense that everybody was saying about her not being a real sister to me also had a hugely confusing effect on me. I was not feeling sorry or pain for myself because I was in denial. To me, Mamgo was not dead and I kept it at that.

People started coming and the service started. The house was full to capacity. People had come to comfort my family. Her peers were there in their numbers and had come to pay their tributes to my younger sister. I sat at the back and listened to what everybody had to say about her and what others had to say to us, her family.

Apparently, a cousin from my grandma's side who worked at the hospital where she died was working a night shift on the night Zona died. I listened to her as she detailed what had happened the night my sister died. She told the congregation of how she had decided to make a turn and go and check on Zona after doing her own rounds just before midnight. This was when she found her praying while lying on her bed. She told us that she didn't disturb her, instead joined and knelt beside her bed and started praying along with her but, as they prayed, she heard that after some time my sister was sounding like she was choking or something; that the words coming out of her mouth didn't make sense anymore. She stood up to check on her and realised that she was not stopping praying, but no words that came out made sense and my sister's tongue looked as if it was withdrawing. She was shaking as if she were having fits.

The woman said that at that point she called out to Zona and shook her, thinking that she would awake and, upon realising that she was not responding to her, she started screaming for the nurses to come and help. She told the people and my family that the nurses and doctors came running and they tried to resuscitate her and while at that they asked her to wait outside. That was how the young angel had departed from this world; leaving us with disbelief, especially after she'd promised me that she was okay. Her own journey had come to an abrupt end, just like that, in the middle of nowhere.

A testimony of how well she had been raised stood out. Throughout the night, both the old and her peers spoke, some encouraging Ande to try and follow in her footsteps and learn from the example that she had set. I felt some false sense of comfort from that. I promise you that nothing can keep my family members completely down. There were two or three instances where everybody laughed because my uncle or his crazy sisters just said something crazy or offside... but I love them like that.

In the early hours of the following morning the hearse came carrying her remains and we as family had to view her for the last time after her demise. I think my mom had noticed that I was not handling this thing well. In fact, she somehow could see that I was in denial, so she asked me to go and view the body of my sister and get closure. Dragging my feet, with my head feeling like I had a tight band around it, I went to view the body. Something sank inside of me and I don't think I got closure as my mom had advised at all. I think it was only the beginning of the whole mess.

I think it was only then that I learnt about her passing. As a result, I don't remember much about her funeral service, I really don't. Maybe I have few snapshots from it, but I can't remember what happened on that day. I remember being busy with my baby. I remember standing at the corner of the tent where the service was taking place. I remember seeing her coffin placed on top of two chairs inside the tent. I remember going to the garden where she would be buried. I remember standing outside the gate of the garden with juice and scones for the people coming from the graveside so that they could have something to drink while the food was being prepared. I remember seeing my cousins whom I hadn't seen for a while when they came and joined me to help with the scones and juice… but that's basically it about the day that my Mamgo was buried.

I do not remember anything about the service and I don't remember putting sand on her grave. Surely that must have happened at some point, but somehow it is not in my memory. I do remember, though, the sense of the deep sorrow in my heart that was caused by Zona's untimely death; the waking up and the realisation that I had the morning I went to view her body while she lay in that coffin. I felt sorry for Ande, granny, mom and her friends. I felt sorry for myself too. I thought about Zitha back in Cape Town; how she must have been feeling, knowing that Zona was being buried but she couldn't make it. I felt sorry for my other siblings: Litha, Lonwabo and Vusi. I started thinking about and remembering other losses I'd had in my life and this brought a realisation that life is short – that I

   A Journey from Nowhere to Nowhere

too could die – and how my children, siblings and my parents could be affected by my death.

Apparently, my brother Litha had told the people during the funeral service that the doctors had drained some liquid from her back. I don't know whether this was drained from her back or the muscles, lungs, kidneys or spine – or where exactly. This liquid, according to my brother, who had gone to see her after that drainage, was about a mugful, or cup if you like, but it was just a black or dark, dirty liquid that had a very bad smell. They drained that from her during the day and she passed on later that same night. This was basically a summary of what I heard from people who were talking about it later in the day

The day went by and, as it was nearing its end, the weather changed and it became windy and it brought some rain and a mini storm. Zona was gone – never going to be seen again above this tough earth. Her soothing voice I would never be able to hear again – even if I cried my lungs out.

The following day came and life continued as usual for a lot of people. Some of my aunts had to go and do the washing of all her clothes, as it is our custom to wash all the clothes of the deceased the day after the funeral. It was difficult for me to face my younger brother. I sincerely didn't know what to say to him and I almost felt like he didn't understand that I was genuinely hurting also. I got a sense that he thought we didn't have a genuine feeling or sense of loss since she was not our biological sister. He felt alone and nothing I could say would make him see or understand how shattered my heart was.

Most people were preparing to leave to their various destinations. I had time to speak to Litha, who had been going up and down. He was the person who'd taken Mamgo to the hospital, collected her body from the mortuary after her passing, built her last resting place and stood before the whole congregation during her funeral to tell them what had caused her death. He was not in a good space and just told me to try and accept what had happened as God's will and let the girl rest in peace. He said being involved in all the preparations had somehow made him feel at peace, even though he didn't really understand the whole situation around her death.

My granny was disappointed, broken, and also was trying to understand and process what had happened. She told me she had been looking forward to seeing Mamgo being a mother one day, successful and happy. "She was a good girl, my child. She had the potential to become whatever she wanted to become. It's a pity that I had to experience her death and burial. The past few weeks have been extremely hard, you know my child. We as old people expect to be buried by you and not the other way around. I am disappointed, but I know that God doesn't lie and as a believer I know that all of us have our times to be born set, as well as our times to die. Zona might have been young, as we say, but her own race in this life has seemingly finished," she said.

It became obvious to me that everyone at home was traumatised by her sudden passing and everyone was trying to make sense of it and trying to move on. This reminded me of my father. A few days before the day of the funeral, he came with his radio to the big house because it was time for a radio programme called *Imiphanga*. This programme was about death notices. Families would submit the names of their loved ones to a specific radio station so that the death could be announced over the radio, together with the details of the funeral.

I'd never really understood the purpose of that programme when I was young but this time around I hoped that Jackie would hear that her daughter had passed on and was going to be buried in a few days. I hoped that she still remembered the name of the place where she'd left her kids. I kept on thinking about Zona's mother who had dropped them off at my place when she was hardly three years old.

"Didn't this woman perhaps hear of her daughter's passing? Would she stay away even if she heard?" I wondered. There were rumours at some stage that one of my granny's old friends had some information about the whereabouts of the two women, but nothing had come of it. I can't remember clearly what the story was because I was still small and this topic was not discussed openly at home. I just remember my granny not being interested in all that, as she deemed it to be pure lies and gossip. What clearly had pissed her off was the fact that the person who had the information was not revealing anything that could help my family trace the two women, but just saying she had met or seen them somewhere.

Then the days were finished and I had to face towards the Mother City again for work. The reality was beginning to befriend us, as friends and extended family members were also leaving.

Things were not easy as one would expect but at least we kept contact with each other. Granny was advanced in age and her eyesight was not as strong as it had been anymore, so she depended on my brothers Ande and Litha to help her with a number of things. My younger brother had a brutal wake up call. He blamed himself for a number of things. He regretted every minute he'd spent misbehaving and troubling my granny and his sister. He was trying to make up for it by taking care of my granny and ensuring that she did not struggle. We became pretty close and communicated more often than before.

ᴏᴏᴏᴏᴏ **Chapter 11** ᴏᴏᴏᴏᴏ

IT WAS EXACTLY ONE YEAR later, in 2010, that my grandmother got seriously injured after tripping and falling inside her house. She had woken up to switch off the lights after the power had gone off and come back again in the middle of the night. This impacted badly on us again, but my younger brother Ande took a huge knock as she was hospitalised for some time. I went to see her in hospital with Litha and Ande and after some time she was discharged. Unfortunately, she didn't make it for long after being discharged from the hospital. May her precious soul rest in peace. Ande had been there with her. He was there taking care of her, together with Litha, until such time as my mother would be able to join them in taking care of her.

During the preparations for her funeral there wasn't really time to discuss our feelings. We had to prepare for the burial. I was helping my brother Litha with getting things in order for a woman who was very important to us. As much as I was hurting, I had accepted her passing differently from Zona's one. I was not able to comprehend the pain that she'd gone through because of the accident. I preferred that she rest, rather than suffering in her old age.

I loved my granny so much and arranging her funeral came naturally, filled with love and compassion. All my brothers were busy, including the last born, from organising the wood to making fire, organising the tents, chairs, getting the cow that would be slaughtered, building and preparing the grave, collecting this and that. The only time I got to see everybody together was at the grave site. That's when I saw Ande breaking down. He was so overwhelmed, and he just cried there, inconsolable. I imagined that that very moment had brought back a lot of sad memories to him. I tried to imagine how he was feeling: the sense of losing all the people closest to you, one after another. The elders tried to comfort him and spoke to him extensively, telling him that he still had family members who loved him and would take care of him.

Already the talk of what was going to happen to him now that my granny was gone was being whispered. I sensed that some family members were scared that he would relapse and go back to being troublesome, since there was no one to take care of him. My father was there at home and Litha was there at home as well, even though they were busy working and doing their own things. The only difference was that they were men; meaning that there was no mother or female figure anymore. Ande must have been seventeen years old already, and he was a grown young man; he did not need a baby sitter. He just needed support in terms of having food and his school needs attended to, and a bit of discipline, so whether my father and my brother came back home late at night wouldn't have been a problem as it hadn't been a problem before. There are a lot of kids who grow up staying with only men and they are just fine.

A family meeting was held a day after the funeral and support was pledged for him. I was among the people who were expected to take the baton from Granny to take care of Ande's well-being and schooling needs. Family and extended family members who lived close by promised to keep an eye on him, since some of us lived far away in Cape Town. Ande was not responding much to the discussions that were taking place. He was just visibly sad, broken, hopeless and alone in his world while everybody was there. I am sure that the reality that everybody would leave and he would have to face those two graves in the garden alone was unsettling for him.

I mean, I am not a fan of going back home alone, without inviting either my siblings or my mother to go with me – ever since we got graves in the garden. The thought of all sorts of things is unsettling for me, and I am this big; imagine how much more so for a young and broken man.

Anyway, the reality indeed came to pass as we left for Cape Town again to face work. I kept contact with him and he was recovering well after my granny's passing. I think we both didn't want her to suffer the way she had and we both had seen her pain and had tried to do what we could for her. I think that's what brought peace in our hearts. That was different from losing the girl who we didn't even know was sick. At least we managed to strengthen our bond and I noticed that every chance that he got he would call me.

We talked about his future. We used to discuss his progress at school and what he would do after high school. He was motivated again, though he was a bit behind with his schooling. I think he was still doing his Grade 7 at the time. I used to tell him that education has no age, so there's no need for anyone to put themselves under pressure; just as long as they know what they want and they work towards that. Also, I never shied away from telling him that no one had taken him out of school in the first place; only his choices. And the same choices he had made to go back would see him finishing his high school and going all the way to finishing a degree one day, and he would agree with me.

One day he called me and said, "Sisi, you know one thing I like about you is that you don't try to make me feel comfortable by telling me lies or covering up the truth. You tell me things as they are and at the same time I have realised that you were never my enemy, even back in the days. You have always wanted what was best for me and my late sister. I love you and I appreciate you, sisi."

"Wow! Wow! Wow! And then! What do you want, *broer*?" I asked curiously.

"*Niks* at all, sisi. I just felt like telling you that," he assured me.

"Somebody is growing up, yeh?" I teased.

Ande just laughed and said, "Yes, sisi".

It was not long after my granny's burial, maybe a few months, that I received a call from a woman who introduced herself as a social worker from Tsolo. She was calling me from back home with regards to my younger brother, Sgwili. He had indicated to them that I was the person responsible for his well-being and schooling after my grandmother's passing. The social worker raised concerns about the boy, saying that the boy was vulnerable and open to drug abuse as he was still trying to recover from using them. She said that, given the history of Ande with his drug abuse and the loss of his sister and granny, he was basically alone at home, as my father and my brother were always at work and sometimes away from home for some days. She alleged that Ande didn't have enough immediate support and that he was still very fragile, and that sometimes there was no food at home and this alone could lead to the boy being involved in doing bad things and committing crime, just to have something to eat.

"Okay," I said, not sure of what this woman was saying to me. I asked her where the "boy" was at the time, and why he would say that I was responsible for his well-being when I was the youngest of them all. I mean, my father was there, and my brothers, and maybe mom too? Why was he saying I'm responsible for him? At the same time I

 A JOURNEY FROM NOWHERE TO NOWHERE

was careful not to say something that would make him feel like I was denying him or didn't want him.

The social worker made it clear to me that I had to make a plan to ensure that the boy was well taken care of and that he had the support that he needed. While we were still discussing this issue I made it clear to her that I lived in Cape Town and I didn't know what the expectations were in terms of this new responsibility. Well, she strongly recommended that I take the boy under my care completely. Yes! Meaning that I needed to find him a school in Cape Town and move him there. I tried to explain my own unstable situation at that time, but she was adamant that I take the boy in with immediate effect as I was now his legal guardian.

This almost felt like a déjà vu. My mother and granny were told by the same social workers to embrace their gift and raise these kids and feed them what they were feeding their own children. Now I felt like I was being subjected to the same situation. I loved my brother sincerely. I'm saying this not because I wouldn't have wanted to take care of him. I already was doing that in one way or the other, but now this woman was saying to me, "Take this boy under your care and send him to school. Make him one of your kids because he has indicated that you are the one who has been assisting him with his needs since the passing of his guardian, which was your grandmother." She was saying, "This boy has indicated that he wants to come and stay with you rather, because you understand him and you are very strict and caring of him."

You know, this was confusing. It was scary and big for me, but at the same time I had to show courage and I felt obliged to do it as I would honour my promise I made to my granny while she was lying in a hospital bed; that I'd look after Ande and that he'd grow to be an honourable man one day, someone of whom she herself could be proud. Well, I told the social worker that I'd think about this issue and that I'd discuss it with the rest of the family to hear their views on the matter. So we agreed that she would call me the following day.

My day was just a mess after that call. I love my brother – believe me – but I was overwhelmed by fear and doubt. I thought of when we were growing up in the village, when people would say that if you went to Umtata you'd literally be swallowed up and consumed by the forces of Umtata if you are not wise. I understood that saying to mean that, if you are a person who's not strong in terms of personality and values, and if you don't know where you are from, and where you are going, then you'd easily lose yourself in Umtata. This kept on playing on my mind and I was now scared that what my brother might be exposed to back in the village would be a thousand times, if not more, in the township. I wasn't sure if I was going to be able to protect him from that exposure.

I tried to put myself in his shoes and realised that I had gone to Umtata to attend my high school, and I did not get swallowed up or consumed by Umtata and that now I was in Cape Town, in one of the notorious townships called Dunoon, and that I had survived all the challenges I'd faced as a young and beautiful girl without losing myself. I realised that it was about the choices that one makes and a huge part of me believed that Ande had already made his choices to leave drugs and go back to school; talk about the second chance at life, right? I felt like it was time I showed what I meant when I said I was his Number One Fan, and when I said I'd support him and that I was proud of him.

At lunch time, I went to my colleagues who happened to be my friends and I shared something like this with them: "Ey guys, you remember *mos* my younger sister who passed on a year ago?"

"Ewe, chommie, we remember her. What about her?" one friend asked with a concern.

"As you know the story, she had a younger brother Ande, who was left with my granny after her passing. Now, with my granny passing a few months ago, the boy was left at home with my father and Litha, my brother that I come after, man."

"Oh yes, chommie, we remember Ande, man. The troublesome one?" Nana asked…

"Yes, my friends, that one."

"Oh God! What has he done this time around, Zowi?" another asked and chuckled to herself. "But you said he was trying to get back in line, *mos* chommie? What has he done now?" she asked.

"Well, I received a call from the social worker in Maclear or Tsolo or wherever the woman was calling from. They want me to move the boy to Cape Town and they want me to assume the responsibility of being a legal guardian to him. Whatever that means," I said with a bit of irritation.

"Yhooo! chomie! What? In all the challenges that you are facing? Do they even know? How are you going to take care of somebody who is just eight years younger than you? A man, *nogal*? With a history of drugs? In a township! Dunoon, *nogal*?" My crazy friend Nana just went on and on. "*Thixo Bawo!* Zowi!"

"It's like putting a goat and cabbage in one place, I tell you," someone else commented… without having been invited into the conversation.

"Haibo! Who invited you in the conversation in the first place?" I asked with some level of annoyance. "Nx! People here like news," I moaned.

"You know them mos, chommie, don't mind them. What are these people saying, na chommie? Do they know how tough things are in your space right now? Or they don't care?" This was my friend who had seen me go through things and she knew what she was talking about. She genuinely asked all those questions because she cared. She was worried about me and about my brother. She had gone through the same experience with her own brother who was born and raised in the townships of Cape Town, but the devil of drugs proved to be stronger.

"Eish! My friend, you don't have an idea," I said. "I'm scared for him, you know, in both situations. Even if I were to leave him where he is and just support him by sending money for groceries for him every month, maybe that's not what he needs at the moment, as he's been through a lot. Maybe all he needs is just family and I honestly don't think that's too much to ask. On the other hand, if I bring him this side, will he be strong enough to resist the temptations?"

We spoke at length about the issue and tried to look at the situation from all sides, but the end result was that everybody makes mistakes in life, everybody learns different lessons in different phases in life, so we were not going to judge my brother because of his past bad choices. Maybe a new slate was all he needed. My friends pledged their support for whatever decision I would make, including helping me to find a school for him if I decided to bring him to Cape Town.

I went home and relayed the news about the call from a social worker to Mama and my sister and they didn't see a problem with him coming up and, because they liked him a lot, they didn't think it was right for him to be staying alone after losing his sister and granny. I was not secretive about my fears and the challenges that we might face with him, but also the possibility of a complete rehabilitation for him. I spoke to my older brothers and they also did not see any problem, as the young man was part of us anyway. So, basically they thought it wouldn't be a bad idea if he came and they all pledged their support. We didn't stay far from each other. Everybody believed that he had learned his lessons and that he was serious about finishing school and putting his life back on track.

At this point, Mom, Zitha and I stayed together with our children, after my marriage failed, so this would make things easy and they would be there for us. The following day, I told my friends that I had considered all possibilities and had spoken to my family members for support and everybody was in. That meant that I would be moving my little brother to Cape Town to stay with us and continue schooling this side. The excitement to have him there with us and the fear of the unknown caused me to have mixed feelings about the arrangement.

I waited for the social worker to call me so I could share these anxieties with her before I could tell her my own decisions. In the meantime, I was worried that my doubts could be seen and translated by Ande as delaying tactics or proof that I too was abandoning him. First, it was his mother, second it was Zona and third it was Granny. I was afraid for myself, but more for him because, even though I'd had my fair share of trouble in my life, I still had my mother. She was there beside me. She supported me the best way she knew, and she never judged me in a single moment of those highs and lows of my life. Also, the other reality was that I still had all my siblings, alive.

The guilty conscience that should have been eating Jackie, wherever she was, was having a field day with me. I found myself being the one who had to be over sensitive; careful of what I said and how I said it.

ooooo **Chapter 12** ooooo

I REMEMBER MY FRIENDS AND ANOTHER colleague driving around with me, trying to find a school for him already, even before the so-called social worker had called back. It was challenging because: one, it was already late for applications; and two, he was already very old for his grade and, considering the crime and roughness that was happening in schools in the townships, no school wanted to accept him to come and do his Grade 9 at the age of seventeen or eighteen, either in Dunoon or in Joe Slovo. These two high schools were the only public high schools close to where we stayed and, due to the strict rules around the feeder areas, we were limited to these two.

My colleague suggested that we go to the Department of Education and ask for assistance. Mind you, I did not have a car and that meant either I had to take a day off from work or we went to the nearest Department of Education office during lunch time, even if we had to use her car, as the department is not open on weekends.

Day one ended without any luck unfortunately; no school wanted to take a seventeen-year-old for that grade. The social worker didn't call back and I won't lie – I was so relieved she didn't, even though I would never have told that to anyone. After three days, the woman called again, while I was at work, and as we spoke I raised my fears with her, citing the very reasons of drugs and accessibility of drugs in the township for an addict or even a recovering one. I had never seen my brother high or experienced any of his mischief; all I knew was from the reports from Zona and Granny, and a few times from Litha. I shared that I had my own challenges and I was finding it hard to get a school for Ande because of his age and the grade that he wanted to do.

She told me that she would send me some documents that proved that my brother was under them and that, because of the circumstances I now had to take over and the reasons that he was still going to do Grade 9 at his age. Well, I agreed then, because I had already taken the decision that I would try my best, with my family beside me to support Ande, as we had done from the day that he'd became part of us.

Now, as my colleague had suggested, we went to the Department of Education in Mitchell's Plain, or Lentegeeu, if I remember correctly. Seems luck was on our side on that day as they helped identify a school that we should go to. They gave us a letter from the Department and advised that I combine it with the other documents from the social workers in Eastern Cape, and that I should also draft a letter to the school as the guardian and take it with to the school.

We went back to work and I had to go back and find my best English to write that letter. I had no clue what I needed to say as a newly appointed guardian. After a few moments of writing and erasing everything again, over and over, I felt that all I was writing there was just making excuses for my brother and all of us involved. I'd never written a letter to a school to start with. I had written all those imaginary accident essays at primary school, where one has to create everything and lie about being involved in some car accident and having a narrow escape, and that had been fun because it was pure imagination, but this one was real. Now I was facing the dilemma of wanting to impress the principal, and also set a standard for my brother.

I wanted the principal to know that my brother was coming from a home of well-mannered and modest people, that he had made errors as a child and how important it was to get a place in the school to finish his Grade 9. I won't take credit for writing the letter to the school because, after writing it too many times and deleting everything again, I remembered that I had a friend whom I could ask to help me draft the letter. Also, the advantage was that he was a teacher as well, so I figured he'd have a clue about what to say to his counterparts. The only thing was that I had to brief him first about the whole story around the school and my brother, but soon the letter was ready.

In a few days' time I was able to go the school that was identified in Dunoon. After the meeting with the principal of the school, they accepted him. The principal had his own – and a lot – of reservations about Ande – like his age, his record and the issue of crime in schools, especially in the townships – but like all of us he said, "Maybe all that the young man needs is support and a second chance in life, and who are we to judge?" All I was hoping and praying for was for my little brother to start over, and that was an opportunity for him to have a new leaf at life. All the while he was still back at home, waiting anxiously to hear about the outcome of all my efforts.

In the afternoon when I got home I found everybody waiting to get feedback and when I broke the news of his acceptance it was like he had been accepted at the University of Cape Town, I tell you. People were happy, but most of all Ande was very happy. I could hear over the phone that he was in the verge of breaking down and crying. His voice was shaking and he just lost words to say to me at that moment.

Plans of getting him the school uniform and his books began and we had people around us in the community who gave some of the things towards his schooling. Eventually, a day came for him to board the bus to the mother city. It would be the longest journey he had ever taken, apart from the one he'd taken with his mother from Johannesburg, when he was still a small baby. This journey would take him over one thousand kilometres. His excitement would die somewhere along the journey and he would even doubt if he'd boarded the correct bus. I forewarned him that the trip would be long and that he would need to brace himself for it. This was not a trip to Tsolo or Maclear, his usual places, or even Umtata if he'd gotten that far when he went to visit at Reni.

On the way he called, multiple times, asking me if it was still far. I think he must have thought we were mad when we used to say the bus travels the whole night when we went home from the Mother City. I thanked God his airtime or battery died – because that was my saving grace. I can still remember, when he arrived the following morning around 10AM, he was just shaking his head in disbelief. "This place is far, yhu!" he said with a straight face.

He was lucky. Our neighbours knew all my older brothers and they embraced him as well. They liked him and encouraged him to focus on and enjoy school. I remember Mom getting him a school bag and someone giving him a scientific calculator and so on. It was a year of new beginnings, full of promise and goodness. My brother was now in a school finally. There were other girls and boys in the neighbourhood who attended the same school, so he soon acquainted himself with them and had people to walk with to and from school. The school was roughly two kilometres from the house, nothing compared to the distances that he was used to back home. He was excited.

On his first day at school, when I came back from work, he told me, "Sis'wam, I think I'm going to like it here. It's good to be back and I'll make all of you proud. I'm going to give it my all, sisi, you won't regret it, and sisi, thank you for doing this for me."

This was the day that I got a chance to talk to him on another level. He was a grown man now and I was interested in knowing his disposition with regards to life in general, forgetting about the losses of loved ones, the issue of his mother abandoning them while they were young. I just wanted to engage him on what he planned to do and what his take on life was – being a guy now and going forward.

He just laughed at me and said, "Oh! *Hayke*, sisi, you want to start now? But it's fine. I guess at some point we are going to have to face this and not avoid it. I don't have children, if that's what you are asking me. No, not yet sisi."

"Heee!" I laughed. "I was not asking you if you have children or not. All I wanted to find out is what your take about life in general is; any dreams of having a family one day, any career plans or aspirations, and maybe your level of awareness about this HIV and Aids? That it exists and also the issue of drugs and drug usage, that's all." Where I wanted to go with our talk was to try and equip him in terms of his new environment and the exposures that he would encounter.

"Yes, sisi, I know the issue of drugs and I have been exposed to it back at home, so I can't expect any difference here in the township. I know that the temptation will be stronger than before and that maybe they won't be difficult to get as well, but I have come a long way now. I don't intend to go back there. I lost my sister without even realising that she was suffering in pain while I was high and if I can't do it for me, then I will do it for her and you guys; my whole family that I still have." That was good news to my ears and I was so happy.

The issue of having a family of his own one day was not something that he wanted to think about at the moment. He said the idea of that was just scary for him. All he wanted to focus on was building himself up first, and getting the people around him to trust him again, instead of adding more people to the equation. Anyway, we laughed about the issue of adding more people to the equation and I said to him that he was a good person and he was handsome too and that I understood the fears as well.

He asked me how I was coping alone with the two kids after the separation from my husband. "*Agh! Wena*, you are still very young to understand," I said to him. "It's not easy but it's doable, as you can see. It's not something that one would wish on anyone, but sometimes things that happen in life dictate what's to happen. What made me live each day was knowing that, whatever issues were in my own life between me and my estranged husband, I would never abandon my kids."

He smiled and said, "*Yha nhe*! I hear you, sisi".

"Yes, little brother, not so little anymore. Whatever you grow up to be one day, never abandon your children. Even if you hate the other parent so much, never let that be a reason for you to not take care of you children, financially or otherwise," I said. "I've always believed that children are a blessing and a precious gift from God, but they come with a huge responsibility. So, to me, the issue of not carrying out that responsibility has always meant neglecting God's assigned responsibility."

"If you say so, sisi," he said in a shy voice.

During his first days of school I'd help him with his work – especially maths, even though I was not the best in mathematics. Shame, maths was not his strong point, I must say. I used to struggle with maths myself, but he was totally hopeless. It was not long before a cousin of ours from the same neighbourhood mentioned that he was actually repeating Grade 9 in another school and suggested that they study together as a team. All sounded and seemed good and

   A JOURNEY FROM NOWHERE TO NOWHERE

from there on the guys were always meeting in the afternoon on specific days. For me this was a big relief. I took it that they both needed some encouragement of some sort; they both needed this.

My mom's shack had four rooms in total, which were a kitchen mixed with the spaza shop and three bedrooms. One of these three bedrooms had its own door to the outside. I used to sleep in the outside room with my kids, but my brother's arrival meant that space needed to be created for him to sleep and we decided that he should sleep in the outside room and that I would move to the inner room to allow him some privacy. That was done, and he was set up in that room.

Even though I knew that my brother had a history with drug usage, I had more confidence in him than doubts about him. He seemed so genuine and sincere in everything he did or said.

At home there was a spaza shop and soon he was helping Mama with packing things nicely in the shop, helping with the customers, fixing the shelves as well. He had visions about the spaza and he communicated them very clearly and made suggestions on how things could be arranged in the shop.

Another thing that I have realised in life is that one tends to be naïve when one loves someone. The reason why I say that is that, as much as one will lose trust in the other person because of one reason or the other, it is not difficult to gain the same trust again when the other party tries hard to be trustworthy again. The issue is, once you forgive the person and he or she gains your trust again, you forget about the bad things that have occurred and you look forward to the good things that lie ahead. This was what befell us in my Ande's case. We loved him dearly and we trusted him. He had managed to win our hearts because he seemed genuine in all he did. But maybe it was a bit too soon to trust him completely.

Soon he started to have access to money from the spaza shop and we did not see anything wrong with that because he was assisting, genuinely and sincerely. If the spaza was out of stock, he would offer to run quickly to the nearest cash and carry in Dunoon to get the stock, and at times Mama would leave him to mind the shop while she went to buy the stock and he would sell things and hand over the money to Mama upon her return.

Around the same time, while everything else seemed to be working well on his side, there were some issues with the school transport for my daughter and as a result I had three choices. I could walk with her to the taxi rank at six o'clock in the morning when I left for work and leave her there unattended until the school transport picked her up at six thirty, as the driver had suggested, because they were not willing to enter Site 5 to collect the kids for school. Or I had a choice of waiting with her and missing my train to work and subsequently losing my job or moving to Dunoon, where it would be easier for her to be collected by the school transport from the flat.

After weighing the options, I decided that I was not going to walk with my daughter to the taxi rank and leave her there alone to wait for some school transport, and I couldn't afford to be late at work either, so finding a flat and moving to Dunoon was the only sensible option. We looked for a flat to rent in Dunoon where I'd stay with my kids, on the understanding that when this young brother of mine came back from school he would go to the flat and wait there with my daughter until I came back from work in the evening. Then we could do his homework before he went back to Site 5 later in the evening. Basically, one needed twenty minutes to walk from the flat in Dunoon to Site 5. It was what everybody who stayed in Site 5 did every day to catch a taxi, as there was only one taxi rank which was based in Dunoon.

Ande did this religiously for a while. Even most Saturdays, either I would go to Site 5 with the kids or he'd come to the flat and then we'd go together to help Mama in the shop. My work was demanding as well; sometimes I would travel to Pretoria for meetings or training and he wouldn't have to come to the flat. After some time I noticed that he had gained some confidence and he would say, "No, sisi, I didn't come because I didn't have any homework," and sometimes he'd skip two to three days, telling me that he was fine and that he'd managed to finish his work in class. This was acceptable to me as Ande was not six years old. I was comfortable and happy with the fact that he was not completely dependent on me with his school work.

There were times when I'd be away for the whole week and I wouldn't see him, but I was confident that he'd settled in well and when I look at it now that could be when all the wrong things started. My mother did not pick up anything untoward and I stopped following up about his work because he was fine. Unfortunately, the few times I decided to do spot checks on his books he would allege that most of his books were in class and the few that he had seemed to be up to date.

As I grow older I have come to realise something about habits, especially bad habits. One, as much as one may try very hard to quit or beat a bad habit, there is always a powerful force, either conscious or unconscious, that will bring it back. Two, it is not easy to face and overcome the temptations. Also, to be quite honest, if one has never experienced addiction, I don't think one really understands how it feels to be addicted to something, be it coffee, a cell phone game, drugs or alcohol, or anything else. It doesn't matter how old or young the person is, and it doesn't matter how big or small an addiction is. It doesn't always have to be drugs that one is addicted to. For instance, I've often found myself trying to quit coffee and I'll be convinced that at last I have managed because when I look back I see two to three months without coffee. But, one silly day will trigger the craving for coffee. Whether it's a colleague at work, or other drivers on the road, or the school. There are so many excuses or reasons to find and by the time I realise what I am doing, I will be halfway through my cup of coffee and then I'm back to square one, drinking an excessive amount of coffee. I don't mean that coffee is bad, but it becomes a bad habit when it's not taken in moderation. So I guess the feeling of craving for something else is similar.

Ande soon found a church (St Johns) that was the same as the one he'd used to attend back home and he started attending. Around May or June, when winter started, Ande and my sister Zitha moved to another house that mama had bought closer to the main road of Site 5. The house was just a few metres across the street from the school. The move was because of the heavy rains and flooding and the nature of the roads in Site 5 during winter. At that time there was still no electricity in Site 5 and there were also no proper streets. When one wanted to leave for school or work it would still be very dark. I remember I used to swear, curse and pray every morning because I would mistakenly have walked into dirty water thinking that it was a dry piece of sand. I always fell into that trap and I'd have water inside my shoes for the whole day.

The other major reason for the move was that by the time one got to the taxi rank or school one would be soaking wet. Moving closer was the best thing to do so that Ande didn't have to go to school in wet clothes. The move entailed him sleeping in that other house, but still doing everything else at home at the bottom of Site 5. He would eat at home and then go and sleep on the other side.

The same applied to my sister. Even though she was working already and had children of her own, she still had most of her things, like her washing, done at home, where Mom was. I also had some of my things there at home. On weekends, we'd be at home full time with the children. The house closer to the main road, and the flat in Dunoon in my case, were just for convenience, especially during the week. Basically, one could say we were still staying together.

I think that Ande noticed that I was busy and he saw an opportunity and took advantage of it. Maybe he saw that my guard was down and I was not monitoring him as I'd used to at first, and maybe that's when the craving for drugs and maybe the temptation or even access to drugs presented itself.

His behaviour didn't change at all. He'd go to school and go back home and help Mama with whatever needed to be done, and then go to friends and come back home soon enough before dark, eat his supper and go to the other house to prepare his school stuff and sleep. At least, that's what everybody believed.

○○○○○ **Chapter 13** ○○○○○

IT WAS ZITHA WHO FIRST raised an alarm about Ande. She alleged that she was missing some things from the house where they stayed. They'd been disappearing piece by piece, and no one would ever know what happened to those things except that they had gone for good. It would be things like small change from the shop, and we would dismiss it and not have an explanation of what was really going on. When my sister constantly raised concerns about the things that were going missing in the house I started confronting Ande in order to find out if he knew what had happened to them. Unfortunately, he would deny ever seeing anything, to the point where he would take offense.

Now, imagine the awkward situation that we found ourselves in. What was amazing was that at home where my mother stayed and where the shop was, there was nothing visible missing. Everything was, or at least seemed to be, intact and we often asked why this guy would target my sister's belongings, especially as he knew that she was struggling as much as we all were struggling. What also didn't make sense was the fact that Ande would deny it to a point of crying, and blame us for suspecting him since he had a history with drugs. I would fall for all this and feel so guilty for even asking him about these things – and you know what? I would apologise to him for even asking him about them.

The missing things grew from small change to a whole pack of Pampers nappies that my sister had bought for her baby. All these things were flying out of the house while it was locked and only the two of them had keys to the house. I asked Mama to keep him away from the shop so that we could try and see what was going on. A decision to split the shack where he was sleeping, so that his room didn't have access to my sister's side, was taken and we did that.

I noticed that he had a lot of friends and that some of them were close family friends or relatives. In the township, anyone who shares a clan name with you or your mom is either your cousin or your aunt. After restraining his access to the spaza shop, money issues became worse for my sister. Even though the house was split, more items continued to go missing from the house until one day it became clear that there was a ceiling board that was loose and that he could enter through there from the other side of the shack. Ande would remove the ceiling board dividing the house and enter and take whatever valuables he could sell quickly to get a fix and close the ceiling board again. Things such as sneakers, money, baby nappies, an iron or kettle were the easiest targets. By the time my sister came back from work there'd be no iron, or something else would be missing, but the house would still be locked.

As family, this was creating a crack between us. Zitha was mad at him for stealing from her and mad at me for not believing her and not seeing through him. Mom also didn't know what to believe because Ande would deny, cry and put us in a very awkward situation where we saw ourselves as victimising him. We were starting to blame and point fingers at each other for not caring, because some of us were not losing our belongings or knowing that our drug addict brother

   A Journey from Nowhere to Nowhere

was responsible for it somehow, even though you hadn't caught him yet.

This was a terrible situation for me as I felt caught up in the middle. I didn't know what to believe. Zitha had a strong gut feeling that it was him: we'd been staying in shacks for a decade and we'd never had any burglary or things missing, except a few times when our shacks were burned down by fire.

Before that mystery could be resolved, I had to travel to Pretoria again. I remember a call I received while I was on training and Zitha told me that she had confronted Ande when her pair of sneakers went missing and out of anger he had responded and said he had taken them and sold them.

"Oh my God, Zitha!" I just buried my face in my hands as if Zitha were looking at me and saying, "I told you so," with some sense of vindication for my having doubted her all this time. My heart sank. "Why is this happening again, Lord?" I kept quiet and listened as Zitha spoke on the other end of the line. Apparently, the police had been called and they took him to where he said he had sold my sister's shoes and other things. They managed to get the shoes and other few items back from one shack where he had sold them, but they did not get everything as he would not say where he had sold the remaining items.

Wow! That was crazy and hurtful. I was disappointed, I was angry and I wanted to call those social workers who had suggested this crazy idea of bringing this guy to Cape Town, in a township, *nogal*. I wondered if my life had to stop so I could monitor his activities 24/7? Or maybe I was not supposed to take care of my own kids because he had suddenly become my old son?

"He is mad if he thinks that I will police him. Maybe he doesn't know me very well then. Really, that would be madness! This person is old enough and I think everybody has tried and given him the benefit of the doubt, or even more than that. The support system he has available is strong and there's no good reason why he is doing this to us and to himself," I thought. I wanted to talk to him and tell him where to get off. It was a pity that I had to hold my horses for a few more days before I could get back to the Mother City.

Those were my thoughts as I tossed and turned alone in a hotel in Pretoria. Some of my colleagues who had helped me while I was running around looking for a school for him were with me in Pretoria and I couldn't find words to tell them what was happening back at home. I mean, it had not been so long ago when I was bragging to them about his progress and behaviour – and now this?

I kept on asking myself over and over again why one person's life would be plagued by such pain. I mean, from being a small boy who was abandoned by his mom while he was still crawling, to losing the closest thing he had, his only biological sibling Zona – and also being captured by the devil himself, the drugs. Unfortunately, no one could answer me.

Anyway, my training ended and I had to go back to the Mother City to face my family and see Ande. He owed me some explanations. He owed my sister a lot of explanation and my mother as well. When I got back home from Pretoria I went to Dunoon to see for myself what was being said in terms of all these things that were missing and obviously wanting to get some answers from my brother. Nobody knew where he'd gone to, he'd be seen here and there, but he was not coming home to eat since the confrontation and confession that had led to the recovery of my sister's belongings.

Now, the reality struck. We had to take stock of the things that could be missing and realised that all my hair dryers were gone. I'd used to have a hair salon a few years back and he knew that all three or four hair dryers were kept in the wall unit there at home. None of them was there. My mom's DVD player was not there. It had been packed in the wall unit since we didn't have electricity and the generator was also not working. All that was there was the box, which was still placed nicely in the wall unit. The inverter was also not there. Unless you specifically looked for them, all those things were not very easy to notice missing.

"I hate to say that I told you so, Zowi, but I did," said Zitha. "Something has been up and you didn't believe me when I told you that."

All I could say was, "Yha nhe! I'm sorry for not believing you. Actually, it's not that I did not, but I was caught in the middle and I didn't know how to react because every time I asked Ande about these things he would deny and even cry. So what was I supposed to do? Yerrr! man! How could this guy do this?" I was angry; I will not lie. I felt stupid and what made me very sad was the guilt trips that he'd put us through when we confronted him about these things. I guess all of us were by that time just trying to establish where we had gone wrong. Fear just enveloped me from that moment. I just didn't know what the future held for all of us, including my younger brother, in the wake of all that had happened. The future looked pretty dim – in fact, it looked like there was no future.

I started picturing all those terrifying stories about having a drug addict in the house and the prison-like life that families have to adapt to. Oh! My God! Was that going to be our fate? Somehow it felt like I had been woken up and just as I awoke someone threw a whole bucket of ice cold water over me. I hate things like this. If it were up to me, all things would be perfect. No embarrassment, no pain and no funny business. I just prefer things like that and I wished everybody could just toe their line. It was a silly thought, wasn't it? Nothing is perfect in this world and certainly no one is perfect either.

I mean, I thought I had been trying my best. I'd bought this guy some clothes to wear, even though some were not new. We were used to buying second hand clothes for all of us, including the kids: it's a normal thing in the township. Even mom and Zitha would buy him things if they found something nice for him. He was adored by our kids at home and they enjoyed playing with him, and my brothers loved him as well and none of them used drugs.

One will often blame oneself, or even mistake the mischief that others get up to for a failure on one's own part. We all do at some point in our lives. I was desperately trying to figure out what we were doing wrong as a family but, because there was nothing, I came up empty handed. There was nothing wrong that we were doing as a family besides trying to live our lives as best we knew how. Also, Ande was not the first child to have grown up in our home. There were a lot of other youngsters, both back at home and in Dunoon, and they have turned out very well and are well respected people in the same community. There was no special way that was used to raise me, my brothers and the other strangers that was not passed on to Ande. He had made a choice to be different – based on whatever demons he was facing.

Now things started to come to the fore. People started to say things. Some said, "The guy is smoking but he's mixing these things". Quite obviously, the smoking issue was without a doubt because his actions and behaviour did not suggest otherwise, but it seemed we were still in for a big shocker.

My brother had not been attending school for some weeks, if not months, now. He'd been kicked out of school on more than one occasion and had been required to bring his parent with to school. Apparently, he would ask some other people in the neighbourhood to go and represent him and tell them that I was away with work and he didn't want to bother my old mom with stress, and he'd give them money or free things from the spaza shop. My brother had never told me that there were issues at school; instead, he continued with his shenanigans until he could not anymore and I guess that's when he stopped going to school.

He would wake up in the morning and prepare for school as usual, and leave as if he were going to school, but we found out that he had become part of a group that targeted other school kids and robbed them on the way to and from school. What was appalling and embarrassing about this whole thing is that none of the kids in our neighbourhood ever mentioned this, not even by mistake. Those he used to get notes from to carry me along, and those who used to write notes for him, were either scared of him or crazy like him, I can't really say.

When you asked the kids about Ande and all the allegations, they'd just say, "Yhoo uta' Ace? You don't know ta'Ace, wena sisi." Because his name was Ande, he had become "Ace" in the township and these youngsters respected him as well because he was no longer a boy: they called him "ta'Ace". We were also no longer calling him by that stupid nickname he used to have as a boy. It would seem Ande had become a dragon that every other school kid was scared of.

So, it turned out that Ande would get notes from them so that when sisi checked his books it at least wouldn't be obvious that he was not attending. His alleged crimes at school related to stealing other children's school bags, calculators and back-chatting his teachers and taking other learner's cell phones. One would have expected the school to call me when there was a problem with the learner, as all my details as his guardian were there, instead of accepting anyone who comes to represent him, especially because his was a special case, but that did not happen. I guess the school didn't know any better: in fact, they would not have known that the people whom he was bringing as his parents were not even related to him. Maybe there is a loophole in the process that the schools use: sending the very child who needs to come with the parent to bring the parent. In Ande's case, he brought to school people who had no connection whatsoever to him, until he got fed up with that as well, or got kicked out of school, whichever happened first. I really don't know.

Meanwhile, Ande was nowhere to be seen. As I tried to locate him, the more strenuous it became on my part. He was avoiding me, and there was an increasing sense of enmity between him and my family. He didn't come home for a while after that confrontation and arrest. No one knew where he stayed. He'd go home to my mom's place, but mostly when there was no one else there, and look for something to eat and disappear after that. One would just see by the mess he'd cause at home that he had been to the house. My sister would hear him coming in the middle of the night with his friends to sleep. They'd smoke and talk till the early hours and wake up early and disappear again. I think the hunger was killing him because Mama was always home during the day and one day he just decided to go home and ask for food instead of sneaking around. But now the problem was that he was saying a lot of things that didn't make sense; as if he were losing his mind or something.

At first, he would get to the house and be talking to himself, laughing alone and sometimes asking for food or looking for food, and then he'd leave. Mama had two kittens at home for the rats that were coming from the rubbish dumping container situated just a few metres from the house. Apparently, Ande would come home to get food and while eating he would say that the food that he was eating was not going to his stomach but to the stomachs of the two kittens. He'd say that the kittens were evil, that the kittens would behave strangely when they saw him, as if they saw a strange dog.

I had asked Mama to let me know when Ande was seen around, because it became clear to me that I was the only person whom he was avoiding, as he was not avoiding Mama. Maybe he was avoiding Zitha as well, but at least he still went to the house to sleep, even if it

   A Journey from Nowhere to Nowhere

was midnight. I'd be in Site 5 for the whole weekend, but he would be nowhere. I realised that maybe it was easy for him to know if I was around because he saw the car. On a few occasions I went home without a car, and once or twice he came and, upon realising that I was there, he'd tell me to wait or give him a break while he walked away.

I just wanted to beat this boy so hard so I could get the anger that I had towards him out, and the frustration that he was putting me and my family through. Apparently, one day he went home and told Mama that he was going to kill those kittens of hers because they were eating his food and, just a few days after his threats, the kittens disappeared. One was found dead behind the shack and the second one was never found anywhere. When he was confronted, he obviously denied it, and he didn't even know that he had said that.

One day he rocked up at home and told Mama that he knew that she was the one bewitching him and that she was in this thing, together with Zitha. He said that they were jealous of the relationship he had with me and that they were stirring a conflict between him and myself. Apparently, when that altercation happened there were church people at home who had gone to have a prayer at home due to these issues. He'd just barged in and told all of them where to get off, threatening Mama in front of them with a knife and telling them he could sort them out in seconds.

I went home that afternoon to collect my kids, who had been there for the weekend, and I was welcomed by this madness. "This is becoming serious," I said, picturing what must have gone down and already my mind was playing a record of what could have gone wrong.

"The pastor tried to calm him down and we also called the police, as we don't really know what he could do," Mama said. She was visibly upset, even though she was not scared of him. I feared for her life.

"Where is he now?" I asked.

"The police have taken him," Mama responded.

"Okay, Mama, you can't fight a person who's high on something that you don't know," I pleaded with her. "We need to do something, fast. He must not have access to this house again because now, if he has started seeing you as his enemy, who knows what's next?"

"Nha! He won't do anything to me. He's just a small boy. I'll bury him alive! Do you hear me? I raised him when he couldn't be raised by his own mother. Instead, she chose to throw him away to other people and now I must be scared of him in my own house? Is that what you are asking me, Zowi? After all the things I've done for this rubbish, now you are asking me to fear him?

"This," she said, pointing at the house, "these four corners are mine and no one will come and do rubbish here, finish and *klaar*!" Mama was just upset and so was I, but what mattered the most to me was her safety.

"I don't mean that, Mama. All I'm saying is that I don't think it's safe to face a drug addict face to face. Either he will injure you or kill you, or you will injure him or kill him. I've read so many cases of mothers who end up being arrested and jailed because of similar circumstances where they end up injuring and killing their own tik-kop children. I don't want us to end up losing you either way, Mama. That's why I don't want you to go through this at all. If only we can find a solution that will see none of you being hurt, that's all I ask.

"Yerr! He says you are bewitching him? Does he know who the real witch in this situation is? Or would he like me to remind him of who the real witch is? What the hell?" I exclaimed in anger. "Why didn't you bewitch him and kill him and get done with him when he was six months old? When he was still crawling? When he depended on you to feed him and change his nappies? This is crazy!"

I was battling to comprehend this absurd treatment of my mother by someone who clearly didn't deserve all our love and sacrifices at all.

"Maybe I should go and visit him in that police station and give him a piece of my mind while he is kept there. Ande is an ungrateful little piece of something, *mos* tjooo!" I was just put out. Completely!

"I don't think you should waste your time to go there, Zowi. Like you said, that good for nothing is high as it is. Now what difference will you make by going there to shout at him?" Mama suggested. "I have called your brother Vusi and told him about what happened earlier today and he said he'll make a turn when he is back from work," she added.

"Alright, what's next then?" I asked.

"What do you think? I don't want that boy in this yard of mine. I don't want to see his dirty tiny legs here, that's all I know," she said. "Plus, the police have advised that we go to the family court with this issue. They said they won't keep him long there, just so he could sober up."

"Alright, Mama. I think let's do that," I said.

⸰⸰⸰⸰⸰ **Chapter 14** ⸰⸰⸰⸰⸰

THE GUY WAS OBVIOUSLY RELEASED by the police when he sobered up and he came back and declared war on my family. After that, he broke into the shop time after another and stole all the coins that were there. Only he, Mama and I knew where that money was and if someone broke in and just went straight there and took the container, it could only be one of us. I tried on numerous occasions to locate him, but he would disappear before my eyes.

My elder brother Vusi met him somewhere and he didn't ask many things: he got him and gave him a few slaps before Ande could manage to get away. My brother was also very angry, disappointed and frustrated by all of this and I want to think that he just saw a twenty-year-old man who was taking advantage of three women, who happen to be his mom and two younger sisters; hence his reaction upon bumping onto this dude.

It seemed as if the problem was becoming bigger. It felt like I was facing a war, a big war that was coming, and I had zero strategy for how I was going to face it. I felt guilty for putting my family through this by agreeing to move Ande to Cape Town, even knowing his history. I regretted everything about him. Vusi beating him up felt like a war had been declared formally now between us and Ande and there was no turning back. I knew from my side that when I said I wanted to choke him or clap him it was just a dream; it was not meant literally at all.

You know you are in trouble when you find yourself talking to yourself and clapping hands out of the blue. If this was a play or a movie I would have said "cut" already, but it was real stuff. I could not understand being played by a child, and by some of the neighbours who enjoyed representing my brother at school in exchange for getting things for free in a spaza shop that they knew very well did not belong to him. This goes to show the extent of evil and rot within our townships and communities.

At this point I remembered that at some point during his naughty spree, he had been uncontrollable back at home, taking advantage of my grandmother and his sister and stealing other people's things; how were we different from them? I was bothered a lot by this because I could safely say that generally we are shy people by nature and we won't, unnecessarily, pull attention to ourselves, especially by humiliating ourselves and our family. So I felt so frustrated and embarrassed by his actions because now he was becoming a fully-blown and feared *tsotsi* in the township of Dunoon and Site 5, and he was known to be my brother and my mom's son.

Everybody knew him very well, so I was confronted by this everywhere I went. At the train station in Maitland when people saw me they'd tell me about his actions and sometimes not to rub the salt into my wounds for some were sympathetic with us; feeling for Mama. My mother was a community leader and she was known to have served the community with humility and dignity. Hence, for someone to just come up and tarnish that image was really bad.

My own home was a place of hope for the community. People who wanted to call the police for one reason or another came to my place. Those who were victims of domestic violence ran to my

   A JOURNEY FROM NOWHERE TO NOWHERE

place, as well as those who wanted to call an ambulance. The injured, either stabbed or beaten up, came to my place for help, and even those whose children went missing in Site 5 and Dunoon at large came. The police would come to my mother's place when looking for a certain address, as did the social workers in cases that involved children who had been missing and those who were victims of sexual abuse. My mother's house was a landmark if people wanted to give directions to either the police or any other help or service that was needed in the neighbourhood.

This happened regardless of the time of the day or night. My mother would wake up and assist. At some point she even served as a police reservist – serving the very same community. It was very painful how things had turned out, where the police would be called to my place not because of any of the above issues that involved strangers but for someone who belonged there in that house – for my mother's son. The place that used to be a place of help for many years now desperately needed help. We were the ones who were helpless in this instance – just like the rest of the people who had knocked at our door desperate for help.

If I went to Shoprite in Milnerton and I met a neighbour, there was nothing else to report except about Ande. Time was not standing still and waiting for us to deal with our issues, as they seemed to be becoming bigger by the day. Ande continued with his burglary sessions at home, time and again, and he was threatening my mom's and Zitha's lives. He said he would kill them. After a number of run-ins with the police and my family, we had to approach the family court to get advice on how to deal with such issues.

The person who invented the saying that goes "one day is one day" knew exactly what he or she was talking about. This one day for me was going to be exactly that: "one day". I was going home to Site 5 as I usually did on weekends, but this time I went alone and I took a taxi. As I disembarked at the bus stop, which happens to be an entrance into Site 5, there were fruit and vegetables stalls along the fence on the outside of Site 5 and on the inside of the gate. There were a lot of people going up and down there as usual; some catching taxis, others exiting taxis like me, others trying to cross the road either to Site 5 or to Dunoon. Cars turned into Site 5 and exited Site 5. The road is more like a freeway and it's quite busy.

As much as he looked like a hobo, I noticed that one of the people seated in front of one of the stalls was my brother, Ande. He was filthy; no shoes on his feet but flip flops and wearing clothes that looked as if they had been dipped in some oil and later hung to dry in a dusty area. I didn't think twice but to go and confront him and hear what his problem was and what he had to say for himself. I felt entitled to some explanation from him. I charged at him and, just as I approached, I heard one of the friends sitting with him say, "There's your sister, *broer*! *Kushubile*." He stood up quickly and put his hands in his pockets.

As I came closer and stood in front of him I greeted, "Hello, guys". He spat a big chunk of saliva in front of me. He looked at me from my shoes up to my head, twice. None of them responded and some just laughed. "I want to speak to you," I said, looking at him straight in his eyes.

"What do you want to talk to me about, Zowi? 'Cos you could have been finished now if you wanted to talk," he said while he continued with his rude gesture.

"*Yhoo hayi ntwana*! The chick wants to talk to you!" Loud laughter erupted again.

"How are you?" I asked.

"Why do you care? Oh, let me guess; so you can go and tell that witch mom and sister of yours? Look here, Zowi! I don't wanna talk to you. I don't owe you anything. In fact, I hate all of you. You guys have messed with the wrong guy. I'm going to teach you guys a lesson, one by one. I'm going to start with these ones who live here in Site 5 and then I'll come to you in Brooklyn last," he threatened, making hand gestures towards me.

"Listen, listen here big brother," I interjected. "Don't be too hasty, nhe! I don't appreciate the fact that you have decided to choose your own path at our expense, but that's your decision, okay? But I'm not going to stand here and listen to you calling our mother a witch."

"Your mom, not mine lady, *utheni*? I know who my mother is. It's definitely not that witch who pretends to be a praying person. That one is definitely not my mother!" he interjected while I was still trying to be all feisty with him. "I don't even know why you are busy stressing yourselves about me. I don't know why you guys pretended as if you cared for me and my sister because even you know you never cared. In fact, you never cared even for your own father and your own grandmother. Let me tell you the news, Zowi, Miss Goodie Two Shoes. You are not my sister. You never have been and you never will be, so fuck off! Leave me alone! You guys are all dogs in that house of yours you call home. Your mother… your mother left your father all the way in the Eastern Cape for him to take care of himself and it's no wonder that even your own pathetic marriage didn't work out. It's because she couldn't be a mother enough to you to teach you manners. You left your own marriage because you are just the same as her. You can't tell me anything, *wena*! You can't fix your own shit and you think you can fix other people's problems? Heh! You think I need to be fixed by you and your lying family?"

Yhooo, by that time he was speaking into my face and the rage in his eyes was like he would spit fire. One of his friends came and stood in between us.

"*Pstek wena*, lighty. What is it now? This is your sister. What are you trying to do now? Yeh? You are really high now, Joe! *Ekse vaya* sister!" he said to me, pointing the way for me.

I was as angry as Ande was, and I pushed this other guy aside and I spoke to my brother. I was also at another level of anger; I could have strangled him. Usually, if I am that angry I am not able to say anything, so I urged Zowi earnestly in a bid to calm myself as much as possible. It was vital that I say something to my brother on that day. It was a do or die day; I might never see him again as he had managed to dodge me for a couple of months already. I believed that Ande needed to know how I really felt about what he was doing for the first time in his life. When he was in the Eastern Cape as a young boy I never really confronted him or said anything to him about his nonsense.

"Oh! So you know witches now? How old are you now? Twenty? You think you just became twenty overnight? Do you want me to tell you who the real witch is? Yhe! If my mother wanted you dead, do you think she would take in an eight-month-old baby who has been thrown away by his own mother, raise him and feed him for later? Do you ever think why your own mother decided to throw you away? Do you even have an idea of who your own mother is?" I was battling to speak, with angry tears cutting my speech.

"*Ewe nangoku*! I know who my mother is. I know my mother is Jackie and I know my father as well," he interjected again. "The problem with you is you think you are better than anyone else. You think just because you have a Polo car you can just pitch here and talk to me anyhow. My father owns a Jeep, dear, so screw your Polo. My father is a Nigerian. He has money; I don't need your pennies," he said.

"So why don't you fuck off and go to them instead of troubling my mother and my own family? Why don't you go to your mother

                         A JOURNEY FROM NOWHERE TO NOWHERE

who's a saint and leave my own mother alone? What's your problem?" I asked, hitting him on his chest. "If you have found your family, why are you stealing from my own family? Why don't you just leave us alone? After everything we did for you, Ande? Really, *broer*!" Things were really out of hand now as I was already in tears and I handled him roughly, pulling him closer to me. The anger had just taken over now and there was no backing down. I kept on swallowing a lump of emotions that I was feeling.

"*Voetsek!*" he said as he pushed me a little. I pulled him even closer and as I made the step the other guy jumped in between again. "I had to take care of your sick grandmother when she was discharged from hospital, whereas you guys sat comfortable here in Cape Town. You are a pathetic shame! Your grandmother died and you were not there and you think you are a better person after that? Huh? This stupid education you think you have makes you see everybody else as fools, nhe Zowi? Where were you with your education when your grandmother got injured and died alone there at home?" he asked.

Ande was taller than I am but because of his lifestyle he had lost a lot of weight and as I got very close to him I felt like I stood a chance – I could beat the hell out of him in the state I was; he was weak. The only thing he could do would be to stab me, otherwise *ndandizombetha* shame.

"Leave her out of your shit! You hear me? Leave her out! How dare you? If you want to do your drugs and all, just let my grandmother rest out of it. Instead, you should be ashamed of yourself. That same grandmother of mine raised you in the church. She build a solid foundation around you and taught you well, but you choose your own sick way, so let her please rest in peace. If you want to be unruly and do your nonsense, no one is stopping you. Go and find a job or something, you are twenty years old anyway, for heaven's sake, and the only person you can blame for your delay in life and *fucked-upness* is yourself.

"It's the same shit you are doing now. Instead of troubling us, maybe you should look for a job so you can feed your addiction. We are not going to work for you. If I ever see you near my home you must know that I'll get you arrested same time and nothing else," I threatened.

All this while the friend was still standing in between us, pleading with me to leave and swearing at his friend.

"Hololo-o-o-o… Zowi, you think I'm scared of being arrested? Please tell her that's my second home, guys. Shame, Zowi, I'm not scared of the police, dear. You can call them now if you want, call the po-po now," he said.

I hadn't even realised that people were watching the episode and someone came up to us and pulled me back and said, "Hey sister, leave him alone. This lighty is high. He can hurt you without feeling anything whatsoever."

I resisted a bit and the guys said, "Please, leave now. You see now, everybody is watching you like a television."

Okay! I turned and left, wiping my eyes as I progressed towards my home. "Vele! Vaya! You don't get to tell me what to do anymore. I'm tired of your shit, together with your family," he yelled as I walked away.

To be honest I was exhausted on the inside. I felt emotionally drained and I was hopeless and a bit afraid. What if he meant all those sick threats? I stayed alone with the kids. My mom was alone where she lived, and my sister stayed alone with her kids and this guy still slept there when he felt like it. I could actually see him killing all of us after that confrontation we had because he wasn't himself; tik had taken over. But regardless, the confrontation I had with my brother was what I had been looking for, even though my heart was bleeding.

"My God! What has happened to this young man?" I continually asked myself and sometimes directed the questions to God, hoping for a literal answer, but none came. The rate he was going at was too fast and I worried that he could get killed any time as his usual business of the day was to rob people. I realised there, in that confrontation, that my brother had met the devil himself again. He was not the soft spoken guy anymore. There was no smile anymore. He was just full of pain and hatred and he was very high! I cursed the day tik came to life and I also cursed those who sold it to our brothers and destroyed our families in the name of making money.

I often wondered why I didn't just delete this guy from my heart and memory and forget about him. He's not real blood, *mos,* and like he correctly said, we are not his family. Why were we going through such pain when we never gave our parents a hard time and such humiliation? I mean, we were not perfect kids nor angels, but this one was too much; he took the crown. My thoughts ran along those lines almost every day.

What made it worse for me was the fact that it affected not only us as his family, it affected the community at large. He robbed people of their belongings, taking their cell phones and money. I realised that I loved this boy then. It was painful but I couldn't let go. I felt like he stood a chance to change. I made some enquiries at work to find out if we could get him a rehabilitation centre before it was too late. I got discouraged by the long waiting list in the public institutions for people who wanted to go to a rehab. The private ones were just not in my league in terms of the fees that one needed in order to get such services.

But the hope was there. I've always had a soft spot for my brothers – in actual fact I am a sucker for all my siblings – and I just realised that I've always been like that. I just don't stop following through on them, especially when I know that something is not right. I usually don't interfere when they are in a good space. With Ande it was no different.

I spoke to my older brother Vusi about the issue and he told me straight that if he saw the boy anywhere near our home he would regret the day he'd decided to come to Cape Town. I was trying to extinguish the fire from many angles and it was really exhausting. I didn't want Vusi or any of my brothers to get injured by Ande, or for them to injure him, and I wanted none of them to get arrested for injuring each other.

"Sisi, I don't want nothing with that ungrateful son of a bitch. The boy has gone too far now and he's pushed us too far now. He can do his shit however he wants, but he must not come and abuse my mother. I'll crush this boy, sisi, really." Vusi did not hide his feelings at all and he had no time to please me or anything.

"Okay, *bhuti*. I agree, *broer*. He's pushing it a bit too far now," I concurred. "Anyway, it's not like we are talking about a teenager here; this person is twenty years old and he should be working to feed his addiction. Maybe it's time we quit treating him like a baby and just tell him to leave us alone and go and find his way far away from us. He is just dragging our surname in the mud for nothing. Nx!" I exclaimed in anger.

I didn't dare mention the confrontation I'd had with Ande to Vusi, and what he had said to me about the whole family, because I did not want to make things worse. Yes, I still protected the very person who was threatening to kill my family: me included in that.

ONE MORNING, I THINK ANDE and his friends were smoking their mix in his room in the shack that he shared with Zitha. I want to believe that they must have left the remainder of whatever they were smoking on the floor next to the bed, and it must have set alight the blankets or clothing items on the floor and boom, there was fire – the shack was burning. Luckily, nobody was inside the shack and it was in the morning already and people had started moving about, going to work and so on. So it became easy for people to notice the smoke coming from the shack. Zitha and the children had not been around at the time.

The unfortunate part was that it was not early enough for his room not to burn, with the fire consuming almost everything in that room, including his books and birth certificate. It was the same birth certificate that had brought about the issue of their true identities, and their new surname, that got destroyed in that fire. We could only see from the remnants that were left after the fire was extinguished. I saw pieces of his school books, pieces of his birth certificate, burned spoons and cracked light bulbs as part of the residue.

When mama received a call that the house was on fire she had to rush there. The neighbours were saying there was no one in the house when the fire started, but that her son and his friends had been there earlier and had left a while before the smoke coming out of the place was noticed by a passer-by.

"Yeah nhe!" was all I could say when I saw all the damage done by the fire – and the proof that this boy was using drugs right there at my mother's place. What kind of disrespect was that? I was just grateful that the belongings of my sister, her kids and the neighbours were not caught up in that stupid fire.

My brother was known on the corners of the streets for his notorious acts. He became feared and apparently he was not shy of anyone anymore. He robbed people of their belongings in the daylight and there was nothing anyone could do about it. I never was lucky enough to see him again after our confrontation that day. The hurt that he brought to my mother and to the family at large was unbelievable.

There were more confrontations with Mom and break-ins at home were becoming a sure thing, especially when there was no one in the house. Sometimes, one wants to believe it when they say thieves can smell things, especially money. It looked like this guy had some sort of intel about what was going on at home as he'd know when no one was there; but what was shocking was his skill in detecting where the money was kept once he got inside the house. I guess the same instinct he used to detect my granny's money was still very strong.

I would have thought that he watched Granny when she hid her money, but it became very clear that in fact this was not the case: the guy was just good at this. I say this because he wouldn't be there when Mom put the money away but he'd get to it anyway. After a few arrests for breaking in at home, a friend who happened to be police again suggested that we approach the family court because, as he said, "You see, Mama, I have been here a number of times and I have had to take your son to the police station a number of times. I have had a chance to speak to this boy to try to understand what his problem is and the reasons behind all these things he does, but to be honest with you Mama, the boy is just an addict, a typical addict, and he is not a kid anymore. He should be studying at some university somewhere or working. From experience I have seen cases where *tikkops* kill their mothers or mothers kill their children because of the stress that comes with having a drug addict in the house. I suggest that you approach a family court before it's too late. Maybe the family court can help; maybe give you a restraining order for this boy. But really, Mama, this boy should find a job and work so he can feed his drug urge."

I supported the idea, fully. "Maybe he is right, Mama." Already, the trauma of all the stories I had read in the newspapers of families somewhere in Mitchells Plain and Delft who had their homes as prisons because of their kids turned terrorists, terrorising them and stealing from them at every chance they got, was too much. There were also stories that had turned out horribly wrong, where a mother or a father had killed their own son because of drugs and the terror that came with that.

I kept on visualising the crazy episodes of this boy insulting my mother and accusing her and my sister of bewitching him and the anger that was displayed on his face on the day I met him. I must say, I also didn't trust myself when it came to protecting my mother, siblings, my children and nephews from our brother turned assailant. What was I to do if he tried anything and I was there or found him there doing something crazy? At some point I would be so angry and curse the day that he was brought into our lives and that, believe me, is a bad point that a person can find themselves at.

Mostly, I blamed myself. Maybe I should have said no to that social worker. I even started doubting if it was indeed a legitimate social worker, seeing that Ande had been able to lie and fool all of us: acting as if he were attending school, having some kids writing notes for him, hiring parents to represent him at school. What if that "social worker" was not real? Could he have…? I thought. No man, wait. There was a letter *mos* from the social worker. It's not possible that he had cooked that too.

I didn't really know the intelligence of this brother of mine but I didn't want to give him too much credit and at the same time I didn't want to make the mistake of underestimating him. Maybe I should investigate this matter further, to get to the bottom of it. I needed to find out if Ande did to us what their mother did to my family. The first place I would need to visit was the school, to retrieve the letter from the social services so that I could verify its legitimacy and then I would take it from there.

My thoughts were making me even more upset. I couldn't help but feel stupid and played from the word go. I shouldn't have agreed to have this boy brought to the Mother City but now it was too late for that. It is no secret that drug usage and abuse is high in the townships of Cape Town and it was not going to get better just because our own recovering drug addict came to the Mother City. I have seen boys from as young as eight years in Site 5 sniffing glue or benzene, using different methods, from juice bottles or chip packets or even plain bread plastic. The vulnerability of these young boys to drug lords or pushers and to crime is devastating. Ultimately, the harsh situations they find themselves in sometimes, if not many times, leads to death – whether they kill each other fighting about the proceeds of crime or get killed while perpetrating the crime. From what I have seen, these boys become so brave and unashamed when they are high or when they want a fix that they can do anything, to anyone.

While I was determined to play Detective Zowi and investigate the situation of Ande coming to Cape Town, the social worker and the letter that allegedly came from the social workers, my own life had not paused. It was also marred by a lot of problems, ranging from being stalked, threatened with death, and worrying about the safety of my kids.

There were nights that we would not sleep at all because some person, who under normal circumstances was supposed to be someone protecting us, was busy patrolling my yard, illegally so. There were mornings I would say a prayer without an amen before opening the door to leave my house for work because I didn't know what awaited me just outside the house. My cell phone was my nightmare: it would ring non-stop between calls and incoming messages. Some days were better and others were crazy, where it was possible for me to receive more than fifty messages in one day. Anybody who was close to me, especially colleagues and friends, had their lives threatened every day. I had to slowly isolate myself from people so that they wouldn't be caught in the stupid crossfire that they didn't even know about. This managed to obstruct my mission to a significant extent.

Mama had to go to the family court alone over the issue of Ande and his abuse, mostly to seek help and guidance. After a few times there was an official who helped her with all she needed in terms of advice on what should happen in terms of the law. The other issue was that Ande was no longer a minor and Mama was told that there was a long waiting list for people who want to go to a public rehab as there were few government facilities. The private rehab centres had to be paid for and are not cheap.

But the first step in all that process is the willingness of the addict to go to a rehab, before one can think about the amount of money involved. It was difficult to engage Ande about that because we had become enemies all of a sudden. There were a number of times that I would spot him from a distance and he would disappear on me between the shacks.

His trademark was a dirty pacifier that was always either hanging around his neck or in his mouth. There were a few incidents of gang fights that he was allegedly involved in in Dunoon. What is funny is that our children were very fond of him and he had not stopped loving them, even though he hated us, their parents. I discovered that he'd see them playing among the shacks and greet them and sometimes give them some money. I even learnt that he would go with them to his smoking corners, where he'd smoke with his friends. As a result, the kids knew his ways and chilling spots, when he was not sitting there by the local shopping centre.

He even exposed the kids to the different types of drugs that he smoked. One day, five years later, my daughter told me that her uncle and his friends used to smoke different kinds of drugs and that is why he was hallucinating, and guess what triggered this revelation? When she was in Grade 6 she was reading her life orientation textbook and she came across this and she exclaimed and said, "Yho! My uncle used to use different kinds of drugs. Mama, come and see". I looked on as she explained what her uncle used to smoke and what the book was saying about the different tools used to smoke different drugs. This was shocking to me as at the time of all this we never knew that he was exposing our kids to all that nonsense. To think that while we were scared of him and his actions, they actually played with him, let alone went with him to his deep corners. Anything could have happened and not necessarily perpetrated by him. There are a lot of horrible things that can happen to kids in our townships. He probably wouldn't even remember that he had been with the kids.

What always kept me awake at night was the idea of him coming to break in at my flat, as he knew that I stayed alone with the kids; or him attacking my mom at night in her shack. Deep down I knew him personally, but I couldn't help it because I didn't know the drugged Ande; the high Ande. One of the family court officials had likened the mind of a person who is high on tik to a rotten cabbage. She described how tik messes up the mind and had even suggested that a restraining order be taken against my brother. She told mom that the issue of hallucinations, visions and a lot of other moods that are triggered by this drug could be dire sometimes. Him suggesting that he was being bewitched by my mother and my sister was a very strong point, as was the killing of our cats, and also the fact that there were small kids at home. She said he could hurt the kids as well when he is on a high.

I was quick to support the idea that he was old enough at twenty years and that he needed to find his own place to stay and get a job to feed his bad habit. He needed to be evicted, even from that back room he used to sleep in; the one he'd recently set alight. So, a restraining order was issued against him. Somehow he became aware of the restraining order and he started blackmailing my mother emotionally: that he was being thrown out in the streets by the same family that claimed to love him so much.

After a while he disappeared. It became clear that he was not in Dunoon. He was not at his usual spot – the notorious corner besides Shoprite Shopping Centre. My mother noticed, my sister noticed and, because I would ask about him often when I visited home, they told me about the loud presence of his absence and also the fact that no one knew his whereabouts.

Every weekend when I visited home I would drive past his usual spot, but he was not there. I was longing to see him, even though it was not a good sight because he looked like a hobo. I was not sure of what I was hoping for. Maybe he would be touched and remember home. Maybe he would realise his problem and come back to ask for forgiveness and a chance to go to a rehab. At home they were also concerned about the fact that he was not around anymore – that I picked up from the conversations I had with Mom and Zitha.

I would ask all my siblings if they had seen him, but none of them had. I must say that family is something else. Much as we were fed up with his silly and bad habits, we still loved this fellow. The reason why I say this is that everyone was concerned about him. Even if we didn't want him to come home, we were more scared of what might happen to him out there. We still wanted to see him. We prayed for his safety every day and we hoped for a change in his life.

While we were still wondering where he could be, one of the guys in the neighbourhood mentioned that my brother had been taken by a police van a few weeks ago. He alleged that my brother had stolen Christmas clothes in some house in Dunoon and sold them and was caught while he was busy selling the clothes. So, when the community members caught him they began to assault him but this guy recognised him and quickly called the police and by his luck he was taken by the police from the mob. Much as this was heavy, it also brought some relief. At least he was safe and alive, although we were not sure whether he would still be in the police custody for that long. I mean, it was already around new year and we knew from experience that he would spend one or two days in the police cells and be released again, especially if no case had been opened against him. Anyway I didn't let the hope die.

On my way to the beach with my family, I bumped into friends of mine who were police, and who also happened to be my mother's ex-colleagues, and I asked them about my brother's whereabouts and they said he was not in the police station. They had not seen him in a while,

"Awu! You guys are said to have arrested my brother *mos* about a week ago, apparently for stealing some clothes from a house in Dunoon?" I asked.

"Oh! You mean that? Eish, that boy! Yes, he was taken from the mob in Dunoon some time, but he was released the following day,

     A Journey from Nowhere to Nowhere

mos. No one had opened a case against him and you know that we can't really keep him there for nothing."

"Mfxm! Just as I thought! Where could he be then?"

"*Haysuka*! You'll never know what these silly tik boys get up to, my sister," the other officer said politely.

Ande had disappeared with no trace. I ran into some of his old friends and asked about him and no one knew where he had disappeared to. After a long while, I was also starting to forget about him when one evening he showed up at home. He came home to ask for help because he wanted to go back home in the Eastern Cape. He said he was tired of the township life and needed a break from all the pressures, drugs, arrests and stress. He said he had been in prison all this while.

Wow! Everybody welcomed this move because the moment we'd been praying for had finally come. Litha back home had also been asking why he didn't come back home. They were waiting and hoping for him to come back home, but no one could forcibly take him and put him in a car or bus and take him there. It had to be something that came from him. After all, he was almost twenty-two years old now. And anyway, even if it were possible, one would have to find him first.

When he finally came back, asking to be sent back home, it meant that someone had to finance his bus ticket home. That could be organised, of course, without having to give him the money. Vusi had to accompany him to Stock Road to catch the bus home. "Huh! A bit of relief, my Lord," I thought. Vusi was also excited and looking forward to a change in this young man's life.

I must say that I was seriously worried about the community back home. In fact, I was scared for them. I was just worried that he'd terrorise the vulnerable people and the elderly and my stomach would turn when such thoughts got to me. But there was renewed hope. I hoped for a change in his life. Believe me, when you have a family member who's addicted to drugs your life changes too. You become hopeless, hopeful, anxious, naïve, and all sorts of emotions overwhelm you. Each day you hope and pray it's a better day. I think it's better if the addict is not a threat to you because imagine praying for a person whom you love and of whom you are at the same time scared. It's crazy, right?

In my life, I had learned that even the person you loved and trusted with your life could turn against you and could actually harm you. I think that's why it was so difficult for me to trust my brother when it came to our safety. Imagine if I, the very person who used to be his favourite sister, was actually scared of him how much more so it must have been for other people who were not related to him?

Before he left, we decided to sit him down and give him a piece of our minds. We didn't want to see his ass again in Cape Town, and he seemed to completely understand. He said he was not worried about Dunoon because he never wanted to see the place either. He said he had been incarcerated all this while for theft and that he didn't want to die and that's why he wanted to go home. I was happy and I could see that the rest of the family was happy too. People were looking forward to the change that seemed imminent.

Ande went back home and he spent some time there without any bad reports.

○○○○○ **Chapter 16** ○○○○○

"**H**UH! MAYBE IT WAS TOO** soon to say anything," I thought when not even a month later my father alerted us that Ande had boarded a bus going back to Cape Town. Yes! Ande was seen by some locals taking a bus back to the Mother City. Apparently, when he'd got back home from the Mother City he'd joined Litha on the jobs that he had locally and he would go and assist him. On the day that he escaped and took a bus he'd told Litha that he would follow him because there was something that he wanted to do at home quickly before reporting for work. That's how he got rid of Litha. He never mentioned to my dad and my brother that he was on his way back to Cape Town.

It was not long after that that complaints started flowing in at home. He was being accused of having stolen some sneakers, some clothing items and some money from people, mostly students who were boarding at my home. We waited in anticipation that he would pitch the following day, but he did not. One day, Mama met him in one of the notorious streets in Site 5. A confrontation ensued when she questioned his return to Dunoon so soon. He just confirmed that he was back and that he hadn't bothered coming home because we had made it clear that we never wanted to see him again. So, he had found a place for himself. A series of break-ins started again and it was clear that he was back for real and that he meant business.

After a series of his stunts, stealing anything he could get his hands on at home, he disappeared again. Some people alleged to have seen him at Langa, around the bus depot, walking bare foot, talking to himself and picking things from the rubbish bins, dirty and wearing old and torn clothes.

There were many different versions of his whereabouts but the one of Langa bus depot was definitely not true. I made it a point that I drove there to look for him and he wasn't there. I saw a few hobos there, but Ande was not there. The story was made as if the person had seen him there a number of times but I never saw my brother there. I'm sure it was not him, maybe a pure lie or a mistaken identity.

When you have a problem in life, you get two types of people: those who share your problem with you sincerely and those who pretend to share your distress while rejoicing in your pain and making sure that they add to your stress by making up stories, all in the name of feeling your pain. My mind kept on telling me that Ande didn't know Langa so what would he be looking for there?

Anyway, sometimes I couldn't even fully express my feelings because it was just a complicated situation. The roller coaster of emotions, and my own instincts, would confuse me. As much I believed I had made the wrong call by allowing Ande to come to the township with us, I sometimes felt like I had failed him in other ways, even though I wasn't sure how exactly. Also, I knew I had to ensure that I trod carefully so as not to hurt anyone in my family.

Some people alleged that he was arrested and was in prison, but we never got to know which prison. The way I blamed myself for his disappearance, I ended up not knowing what to do. I just prayed an endless prayer to God to protect him and I waited for a day that he'd pitch and say he wanted to go back home to the village again.

My family waited for that day too. Litha always said the boy should come back home, period. He believed that there was no place like home. Even if one makes a big blunder – home is always home. But where was the boy? I wished it was easy to just forget about him altogether, but it was not easy. There were a lot of things that would remind me of him. Anyway, my cheeky self would say, "Mfxm! This guy brought this upon himself, *wena*. You are just bothering yourself about someone who is having a good time. Really, now! Can it really be the best time of his life? I'm sure God has a better purpose for his life, man. I can't think this is it about my younger brother..." My thoughts were just all over the place.

I've heard people preaching that we all have different journeys, and that every one of us is on his or her mission, but what bothered me the most about Ande was how unbelievable his own journey of life was. I mean, could it be that he was made to suffer throughout his life? Was he to have a life without peace at all? It doesn't matter how much you have sinned, I don't think one person should face such pain. I mean, we all sin at the end of the day.

Remember that, even though my sister had passed away about five years ago, I had not given myself time to mourn or deal with her death. I always managed to shelve it somewhere and a year after her death my favourite person, my grandmother, passed on and that also was a difficult incident for me to deal with it and to heal from completely. It still traumatises me how she got injured and eventually died a few weeks after that. I sometimes wondered if my granny and my sister were guardian angels watching over me, us, and could see all these mixed feelings and confusion. Anyway, it always seemed like there was nothing much one could do about the situation except to pray and wait for the Lord to intervene.

Somewhere in 2015, rumours of Ande being around in Site 5 resurfaced again. He was alleged to have been seen in Dunoon and in the vicinity of the Shorprite Mall in Site 5. By that time, my mother had already moved to Chartsworth. My middle brother Lonwabo and his family – two kids and his wife, Nosisa – took occupation of the house in Site 5 from Mfuleni. Lonwabo had found employment in one of the malls in Table view and it only made sense that they move and stay closer.

It was not long after the rumours had been doing the rounds that Nosisa also spotted him walking past the house. He was not so used to Nosisa as they had stayed far away. Ande started coming to the house in the name of just passing to greet. After some time, he started hanging around in the neighbourhood and eventually worked his way back home.

He would go past and spend a few minutes chatting with Lonwabo's wife, and playing with the kids as well, and leave after that. Lonwabo and his family had never really experienced all his nonsense because of the fact that all the drama was happening in Dunoon while they stayed in Mfuleni. They'd used to hear about the things happening there over the phone. My brother's wife would always be at home as she was not working, and my niece who was also still too small to attend school would also be home.

Ande has always loved kids and kids loved him too. Sometimes, Nosisa would see Ande entering the house carrying my brother's son or running and chasing him. This is when she started being comfortable with him coming to the house and started offering him food when he came. When I heard the news, I asked Nosisa if she was sure of what she was doing because I lacked trust in Ande. I was relieved he was back and alive, but still had a lot of reservations about him. She told me that he looked neat and sober.

Lonwabo found him at home a few times when he came back from work. He told them that he was staying somewhere in Site 5 with a homie who was his friend and that he had got a piece job where the homie worked; meaning that when he passed by there he'd be on his way from work in Parklands. I was happy with him working so that he could fund and feed his drug cravings without having to terrorise the community.

One day I visited home to check on the family, as my father was there as well. It was then that Lonwabo's wife told me that Ande had given her some money to go and buy some vegetables for the house. "Why would Ande give you money to buy vegetables for your house? Since when?" I asked her. She shrugged her shoulders and responded as if she wasn't sure what to say to me.

"Hey, Zowi, he was contributing because I often give him food to eat when he comes around."

"Wow! Is that it? And you believed that?" I asked whether my brother knew about that information and Nosisa said she had told Lonwabo about it and he'd never responded or commented on it.

I cautioned her about Ande's actions and behaviour. I had discussed some of the issues in the past with Lonwabo, and shared the frustrations, but I was not sure to what extent he had discussed or shared these challenges with his wife. There were many instances he would be fuming on the phone and wanting to come to Dunoon but couldn't make it due to lack of employment. I made it clear that I was not asking her or them to hate him, or not give him food, but I warned them that they should be careful of what Ande brought to the house and gave to them.

Nosisa became very fond of Ande and she often told me how funny he was and how she and her kids enjoyed his company. He would tell her all about his mischievous acts. How he used to outplay his drug addict friends. It was no secret Ande loved children; I knew it from my children and other children in the neighbourhood. It became a practice that Ande was permanently eating dinner at my brother's place. Sometimes he'd give them money to buy meat and sometimes vegetables.

One day I called Lonwabo and asked him if he was aware that Ande would sometimes give money to his wife to buy things for the house and he said that he knew. He said they had decided to give him food when he came around and, because he said he was working, they didn't have a problem with him contributing towards something to eat. I just cautioned them that, while I didn't have a problem with them giving him food, as I would do the same if I were in their shoes, my worry, or concern rather, was about the alleged job. I did not want Lonwabo to find himself in conflict with the community or the law because he accepted things or money from Ande.

My other concern was that, if Ande stayed with a friend or homie, then why would he eat dinner at my brother's place almost every day? I asked Lonwabo if he had given himself time to confirm what Ande was saying about having a piece job and where he stayed, and it turned out that he never had. I was just worried that one day they'd see people coming to their home looking for Ande or their belongings. I was worried that in his journey he would point at them and say he gave them the money from selling stolen property.

As if I'd known it was going to happen, one day, late in the evening, Lonwabo had just got back from work and his wife was busy preparing dinner, when they saw a car parking just outside the yard. Four men got out of the car and came straight to the house. These were taxi owners and drivers from the taxi rank in Dunoon. They were looking for an engine that was allegedly stolen by Ande. He had pointed them to home when he was caught. Exactly my fear! I had known this nonsense was about to happen. I had learned Ande's tricks and I could just see through his acts. Fortunately for Lonwabo the taxi owners were not violent and they listened to my brother when he explained the story of Ande and what was on the ground regarding him and they left, taking Ande with them and threatening to sort him out until he told the truth about the whereabouts of the lost engine.

When Ande resurfaced again after a few months, he downplayed the incident and laughed about all that had happened the last time he was seen at home. I would listen to my sister-in-law laugh about all the crazy things Ande used to tell her; from stealing, being caught, stealing identity details of his friends so he could sell things at the scrap yard, as his own had been destroyed in the fire a long time ago. I never saw anything funny about such things. There were a few times I almost bumped into Ande at home, but just as I parked the car he would leave.

One day I asked him not to leave on my account as I was just passing to check on the family. He stayed for a few minutes and tried a conversation with me. He asked me why I hated him so much. I asked him to change the question around and ask himself why he hated himself so much.

He said, "It's fine, but one day is one day".

I said, "Sure".

That was the last time I ever saw my younger brother. That was our last meeting, the last words we spoke to each other. I think I'd just had enough of being blackmailed by this young man. I would wait for that one day he was talking about.

Ande disappeared again.

∞∞∞ Chapter 17 ∞∞∞

IT WAS OCTOBER **2016,** IN Mahikeng in the North West Province. I had relocated from the Mother City just a few months before to take up employment in this town. This was a big and rather strange move from the beautiful city to a small town, but I was okay with it. I needed the peace of mind that came with living in a rural area. It was a Monday, around lunch, when my phone rang at work and I picked up the call. The woman identified herself as someone who used to stay in my neighbourhood in Site 5 and said she had seen somebody who looked like my younger brother Ande lying dead in the sports field in Dunoon, but the police wouldn't allow them closer so she couldn't confirm for sure if it was him.

"O-kay thanks, but I'm not around to be able to come and check," I said. "Wait a second, sisi, where is this exactly in Dunoon? Which sports field are you talking about?" I asked this question as somebody who didn't know that there was only one sports field famous for being a place where thugs targeted their prey early in the mornings when they went to work and late in the evenings when they came back from work. There are a lot of people who have lost their lives in that same sports field.

"It's the one and only sports field behind Sophakama Primary," she responded.

"Oh yha! You are right. Thank you, sisi, I really appreciate your call." I remembered that it was not long ago, one fateful evening when Vusi had been found in the same sports field, robbed, beaten with stones and golf sticks and left there to die. Had it not been for the couple that went past and saw him lying there covered in blood, and carried him to the street where he could be seen and get help, he would have probably died there as well. Maybe his body would have been found in the morning by those who went to work and passed through the place.

Immediately, I called my sister Zitha, but her phone was off. I called my middle brother Lonwabo; his phone was off too. Eish! I called Vusi, but he was not picking up.

"Alright, let me try and call Lonwabo's wife. The phone rang for a while but she was not picking up either. "Come on! Pick up, lady, please," I mumbled to myself as her phone kept ringing. Eventually she picked up.

"Hello dabs," she said.

"Nosisa, are you guys well that side?" I asked.

"Oh yes, we are well, dabs, besides this thing about Ande. People are saying someone who looks like him was seen lying dead in the sport's field in Dunoon. Now the problem is that your brother had already left for work when I heard, so I want to wait for when he comes back from work. Then we will go to this other woman who also alleges to have recognised Ande to get more information, because no one is really sure if it was him," Nosisa explained politely.

"Ey! Somebody called me this morning, telling me the same thing, and that's the reason I am calling. I don't know the woman who called me and I can't even remember what she said her name was," I said.

"Okay, it must be her, dabs, for sure, it must be the same person. Apparently she used to stay here in the neighbourhood. Eerr… the thing is I couldn't even go there because when I heard they said the body was already taken by the pathology services," she explained.

"Okay then. I will wait for you guys' feedback later, when your husband is back from work. Please keep me posted," I appealed to her.

Lonwabo came back from work and was received with the news of Ande's passing and his body being found in Dunoon sport's field. They went to Dunoon to see the woman who was understood to have seen my brother's body. Apparently her husband confirmed having seen the person as well and said that he looked like my brother. Later in the evening, some community leaders from Dunoon, together with a few from our neighbourhood, went to the house to tell Lonwabo that a young man believed to be my brother Ande had been found dead that Monday morning in the sports field in Dunoon and that, as leaders, they had come to formally report it. They said people on the scene had identified him as my mom's son.

Eventually, I managed to get hold of my sister and she confirmed the news but had reservations. She felt it could be a mistaken identity. This was because Ande had not been seen in the area for a while. So, appearing dead now didn't make sense at all. Some said there were two bodies found on that field that morning, one without a head – which was later discovered across the railway – and the second one was my brother with visible stab wounds, as if a panga had been used to attack him. Some people who went to the scene even suggested that he might have managed to escape from his killers but later succumbed, fell and died, where he was later found in the morning by people going to work.

All these were just rumours and speculations about what could have happened to the person who was found there. So I gave myself a false hope – that there was a big chance it was not him. I called my mother and her phone was also not going through. Anyway, I slept with that false hope and I prayed very hard that it wouldn't be him. I didn't want the dude dead. I so wanted him alive, changed, and I wanted him to beat all the odds and become someone of whom he could be proud. I wanted him to tell his story and motivate others who would hear his story. I had pictured him in life – successful, with a family of his own and beautiful kids. Dying was not part of that picture.

The following morning, the first thing was to try Mama's phone again and this time she picked up. "Mama, I have been trying to call you since yesterday but couldn't get through," I said.

"Yes, dear, my phone's battery was flat," she explained.

"Okay, Ma. Did you hear about this body that was found in Dunoon yesterday morning?" I asked.

"Yes, my girl, I heard. Nopasika called me and told me that she had seen the body of Ande being removed by the pathology at the sports field in Dunoon yesterday. She just called me this morning," my mother responded in a rather low voice.

"Awu! Is it him for sure, Mama?" I asked.

"Ey, Zowi dear, it looks like it's him; she was sure. Remember that she is a community leader so the police could have allowed the leaders closer, I don't know, my child, but she was sure. The other thing, Zowi, is that they know Ande well *mos*. It's been a while now since they saw him, but he was known by a lot of people."

"Oh! My God! Alright, now what happens next?" I enquired with a bit of concern because I knew that this was going to be a complicated process.

"You ask again…Ey, Zowi! I don't really know, my girl. We'll see," my mother responded in a soft voice. I understood her very well. I also did not have the energy that would be required for this process should this dead body really be that of Ande.

"Okay, Mama. We'll talk later then, bye." As I hung up I knew that it was him but I still refused to accept it, I guess just for the sake of refusing. Maybe I was trying to hide myself from the reality – our reality. It couldn't be that so many people would mistake his identity, and in that case it was just a matter of time before we'd have to meet as a family and discuss the way forward. It was exactly that way forward that shook me to the core because it was non-existent; there was no way forward.

Anyway, the following day Litha back home called. As my phone rang I looked at it and I thought to myself, "If Litha calls me, then it means he knows something," and I found myself quickly being forced to allow my false hope to dim by the minute. "Hey brother! How are things?" I asked in a low voice already. I knew what this guy would say.

"Sisi, we are well, man, besides this thing of Sgwili. I'm hoping that you know *mos* that this boy has been killed in Cape Town." I listened as he spoke softly and slowly as usual. "I don't know how, my sister, but his friend, who is our homeboy who stayed with him somewhere in Dunoon, called and told me that he had died from being stabbed. He is not sure what happened but suspects the mob justice or a fight amongst his groupies. Sisi, are you still there?"

Litha just went on and on. "Mhmm! yah nhe!" I sighed deeply as Litha continued to speak. "Yha! I am still here, brother, I'm here, and I'm listening," I assured him.

"Okay sisi, thanks man. So, as I was saying I'm calling to…"

"Litha, is he sure that it's him?" I interjected.

"Yes sisi, it's him. The guy went and checked him. He said even the clothes were his."

"Yho! Okay, I see," I said.

"So now, sisi, I was calling because I wanted us to discuss how we are going to get his body and bring him home, you know? He needs to come home now and rest. What's done is done," Litha continued and after that he paused. There was a bit of silence from both of us. I wasn't sure about what to say.

"What do you think, sisi? Mna, that's what I think needs to happen now. We don't have control over what happened in this boy's life but now it's ended, he needs to come home to rest beside his sibling Zona." Litha spoke with compassion, trying to emphasise the importance of taking the body of Ande back home.

"Eish! I don't know, to be honest with you, Litha. As for me, I no longer had him on my policies and I doubt if any of us has, but I will have to check." What made things even worse is that, even when we knew he could die anytime in his line of duty, we couldn't even provide for such an eventuality as his birth certificate had got burned in that stupid shack fire that he'd caused together with his stupid friends. Also, my policies where I had insured everybody had lapsed a long time ago. Given his behaviour, I doubted if anyone had any interest in anything to do with him, as we were *gatvol* of everything that had to do with him. And now, this is our reality.

"Yeerrr man, Ande!" I exclaimed in great exasperation. "Where on earth did this person come from really?" I enquired.

"Sorry sisi. You know that we didn't know the answer to what you are asking while he was still alive – we won't know now. Yerr! This lighty has caused so many problems man, sisi, but what is important now is for him to come home and rest beside his sister. We can't run away from the fact that he did rubbish, but we just need not focus on that right now," Litha added, trying to calm me down.

"I mean, Litha, where is the money going to come from? I don't have money stashed somewhere waiting for this shit. Please forgive my language, *broer*, but I'm just angry now," I burst out at poor Litha.

     A Journey from Nowhere to Nowhere

He was as calm as he usually is and he asked me to calm down. "Have you spoken to Vusi and Lonwabo? What about our father? What did they say?" I asked – one question after the other.

"Err.. I tried callin…."

"Nx! My policy that had covered him lapsed long before he went astray and there was nothing I could do about that as circumstances dictated at the time. At this moment I don't have money and I don't even know where one could borrow it from," I interjected again while he was still taking his precious time to answer my questions. He was just too slow for my liking on this occasion.

"Alright sisi, I do understand. I just want us to try and find a way of bringing him home to be buried beside his sister, please Rhadebe," he pleaded sincerely.

"Okay brother, we'll see. Let's talk some other time. I have to go back to class now. I am in Pretoria attending a course for six weeks, so it would be wise to contact me after five o'clock in the evenings. Also, please remember that this person alleged to be Ande still needs to be identified. It could be him or it could be a mistaken identity. We could be stressing for nothing here." I still added that part.

I was not hurt or emotional about his alleged death for some reason. I was not angry. I just continued with my life as if nothing at all had happened. I knew that I didn't have the money that would be needed to bury the guy if he was really dead, and no one in my family did have. No one still had an active policy for Ande; mine had lapsed along the way when my own life was off the tracks and, to be honest, I couldn't expect anything different from anyone else. I mean, the guy messed up all of us and we had written him off, out of our lives completely to the greater extent. At least, that's what we thought or pretended to feel, and it was understandable that there would be such consequences.

I had an opportunity to talk to my other siblings in the Mother City and hey, people were angry and also put it very clearly that they didn't have any money and certainly didn't care what happened to his body now that he had died in his chosen line of duty. I felt like that too – to some great extent. I fully agreed with everyone, but somehow my heart was saying something else to me.

I wondered what my grandmother would have said to me under these circumstances. What would she have suggested we did? I really needed her wisdom in this instance. "Ey! Nontuli! I miss you and I need your wise words in this case. Even if a person did you wrong you'd know what to do if the person came back and was in trouble. I wish you had not had that accident in 2010; maybe you'd still be alive now. Maybe we wouldn't have got to where we are today. I miss you terribly, *Msuthu*. I miss you."

It was then I felt tears streaming down my cheeks and making their way to my chin. I then visualised how she must have suffered, in pain after her accident. I visualised the talk we'd had when I visited her in hospital. How her eyes lit up when I told her it was me, Zowi. Her eyesight was not good anymore and it was difficult to see that it was me. Litha had been telling me that her eyesight was becoming worse by the day and that if anyone entered the house she would ask if that person was Zowi. Litha had also told me that he thought that my grandmother was missing me because, even before the accident, my name was always on her lips. Sometimes she would call him by my name and that got worse when she was hospitalised.

I sat beside the mirror in that hotel room, reminiscing about all that had gone down in the year 2010: the year that my granny had died. How I had kept some information from her, especially about my hostage situation that almost got me killed and that I'd found myself in just a month before she died, because I feared it would kill her. I thought she was going to pull through from that accident. I cried alone there until there were no tears coming out and I dozed off and slept then and there.

The reality about Ande's situation is that we didn't have any document to say to the authorities this is my brother, or this is my son – here is proof. There were no identity documents and we did not have the same DNA, so even if we'd wanted to prove a relationship we couldn't. Also lastly, we didn't have the means to take him from Cape Town to Tsolo, my home village in the Eastern Cape. There were even thoughts among us, as well as suggestions, to just leave him there, wherever his body was. If it was him for real, leave everything to the municipality to see what to do with him.

I was sold on these suggestions and ideas. I wasn't able to take responsibility for how this guy would be buried. I was in no position at all in terms of finances. I was not even on the ground to maybe check if there were friends who could lend me some money – at least fifteen thousand Rand, or ten minimum. Hearts were heavy and people were angry. I was angry too, and I didn't care; I didn't care what happened. At the end of the day I consoled myself that one could only do so much.

My father had already been in Cape Town for almost a year when all this happened and, when I asked him for his opinion on the matter, he said it would be the right thing to do if we could take him home, but there was nothing that could be done as the circumstances were not in favour of that. My mother told me straight that she wouldn't be trying to crack her skull thinking about that. There was nothing she could do.

Vusi wasn't shy about his feelings either. He told me, "Sisi, he can go to hell. I didn't send him anywhere. If he was willing to be a child and go to school where we sent him, we wouldn't have to talk about this today. The municipality will see what to do with him.

They always do about people who don't have relatives to claim them, anyway."

I wasn't sure whether what Vusi was saying was a fact or if it was just out of frustration, but I concurred with him on that one: the dude could go to hell. This seems the easy way out, doesn't it? It sounded very easy when compared to the stress of having to figure out how he was to be transported back home. Paying for his bus ticket the last time was the easiest and the cheapest solution, and I didn't mind paying for him. This was a different transportation this time around. It's a fact that it is way better to pay for a warm body than a cold one. The difference in price is a couple of thousand Rand.

I was shy or embarrassed to come out and say that I was not really concerned about what happened to this dead brother, but the reaction from my people gave me some confidence. It was not even a matter of putting together our small contributions and taking Ande home. We were flat broke and there was certainly no interest in doing it. It's not as if I had hired him to take drugs or something, or as if I had something to do with his drug problem anyway. Litha didn't call again and I forgot about Ande and the stress that came with thinking about him.

In Pretoria, it was lunch time. I was walking with colleagues towards the dining hall and we were talking about the issue of drugs and their impact on families. Suddenly, I remembered that I had a brother who could be the man lying in the morgue, due to tik addiction. I was not going to say it otherwise: if he hadn't used drugs and hadn't had an addiction, he would have stood a chance. I would not be walking here wondering if it was him or hoping it was not him. I would be sure that he was either in class in some university or college, or even at work, for that matter.

It is not easy to lose someone, you can be separated from a person due to certain circumstances or situations beyond control, but

     A Journey from Nowhere to Nowhere

death is too permanent for my liking. If a person is dead, there is no talking with that person and that's the scariest part for me. While my brother walked around, spent some nights in police cells, jail, under the bridge and everywhere else, there was still a chance to have a conversation with him, but if he's dead, that's it!

"Guys! Now that we are talking about the issue of drugs and families… Actually, as I'm walking here with you, I'm hoping for news from home. I'm waiting for confirmation if it's indeed my younger brother who was found dead in some sports field in Dunoon a few days ago. There's a high possibility that it's him. He was on drugs and out there, robbing people and stealing other people's things. I'm not proud, but in pain, and I will not say otherwise. We have not seen him in a while now, since he left home and became a street person, and a body was discovered on Monday morning with suspected stab wounds.

"Now, some people have come out and said it was him but we as a family have not been able to officially go and identify the body as yet, hence I'm saying 'could be', because I'm still hoping for good news. The way my heart is so cold, I don't even know myself anymore. I'm not feeling anything except a bit anxious. In fact, I don't even know how I'm feeling. Maybe just frustrated. So once the family has identified him then we'll know for sure." I concluded.

Everybody was just silent, probably listening to my narration or feeling sad for talking about something that one of them was actually experiencing at that present moment. One of the ladies spoke up eventually. "Eish! So sorry to hear that, Zowi, that's very sad. We'll keep you in our prayers."

"Yeah, man! Let's hope that it's not him," said another colleague.

I realised that the me time I'd had while I was sitting in that hotel room had left me with two hearts: one that wanted to leave everything with regards to Ande and forget that he ever existed, and one that wanted to do something to help ensure that he got identified and taken back home for burial, even if there would be no formal or normal funeral for him. I loved the dude, but the anger I had towards him was a huge monster and it would swallow anything good I wanted to think about him.

When Litha called one evening, I told him that I wasn't able to help with the situation of Ande. "No shame Litha, I have thought about this issue and I don't see how it's going to work. Why don't we leave everything and try and forget about him? I mean, Ande had made a choice. He had not been living with us anymore. He had come out as our enemy and stole a lot of things from us. He called us names – witches and liars and all. Even threatened our lives. Now he is dead, must we worry still? Ai! Litha I don't think so, *broer*. He's not even one of us at the end of the day. We just did what we had to do to raise him, but he chose his path apart from us at the end of the day and he knew that very well. Maybe that's why it was so easy for him to hurt us like that."

I tried to persuade my brother, hoping that he was going to see things the way everybody else was seeing it.

"I understand, sisi, but we cannot be like him and behave like him. We don't smoke what he was smoking, sisi. The boy was troubled, sisi. He has caused a lot of damage even here in the village. He has hurt us too here. Also, sisi, please I ask sincerely, let's do it for our granny and his sister Zona. Please, let's forget about him and do it for those two people. Our grandmother would never have a peaceful rest if we throw the body of this boy away, sisi, and you know it best out of all the people. She would turn in that grave, sisi. I know that you are hurt and angry, sisi, but I'm hurting too and I'm angry too." Litha spoke very softly and clearly.

"I'm not hurt," I interjected while he was still talking. "I'm angry. His behaviour is very expensive man – emotionally and otherwise

– and now it requires money that we don't have, Litha. Like I told you, we do not have any of his official documents like an identity document. His birth certificate got burned with the shack. How on earth are we going to be able to release his body if we were to release it? Answer me now."

"Eish, sisi! This is painful, but I get you. Has he been identified at all?" he asked.

"Not yet. We still need to ask Vusi and Lonwabo or even Mom to go and identify the body, remember? If they will be allowed without anything in terms of documentation pointing to the deceased. Hear me properly here, Litha, you know that if I had the means to carry this out I would, without a complaint. The problem is that I don't have the means and there's nothing I can do about it. I'm at a stage in my life where I can't get money, even from the bank, so you can imagine," I tried to explain further.

"Yhoo! Okay, sisi, let's talk some other time. I want to check if I cannot find a copy of his birth certificate here at home and maybe send it to Lonwabo so that they can take it with when they go to the police station."

Hardly a few hours had passed when Litha called again, this time telling me that he had found a copy of Ande's birth certificate and that there was an undertaker leaving from Cape Town in two days going back home and he had arranged with it to bring Ande's remains back home. Obviously there was a price to pay, even though it was a reduced amount, quite significant compared to what it would have cost had a taxi (quantum) taken his remains home. He said he had some of the money but it was not enough.

"Eish, Litha! How much are we talking about?" I was looking at the subsistence allowance I was getting from work since I was attending training, trying to see if I could maybe make something out of it. In the meantime, everything had to be done quickly now to try and not miss the opportunity that was being offered by the undertaker.

I asked my mother, together with Lonwabo, to go to the local police station to enquire about the body that was found in Dunoon in the hope of finding the detective allocated to the case. This exercise would provide information about the whereabouts of my younger brother's alleged body and allow the family to identify him and be sure if my brother was indeed dead or it was just a mistaken identity. I was hoping that it wouldn't be him so that we could go back to our normal lives without having to explain how broke we were.

The second heart that I had was much stronger than the first. I wanted to help Litha and not Ande. I made up my mind that I had to give him some of my allowance so that he could add to the money he had gathered to take the dude home. I knew that Litha wouldn't let that go down. He was not going to bend towards what I was preaching to him. A way had to be made to take our younger brother home and that was his conviction. Hence there was already an undertaker on standby. I told him that I would send the money to him so that he could add it to the money to pay for the undertaker, but the rest he needed to find by himself.

I told Mom and Lonwabo that there was an arrangement with an undertaker already and it would leave in two days' time, so we needed to try and move swiftly with the process of identifying the body. There was no resistance from their side and they agreed to go and identify the body and assist with the rest of the process of getting his body. What was important was for us to know what to do in terms of claiming the body if it turned out to be Ande. For me, I prayed to God that it was not Ande who was lying dead in a government morgue somewhere, but unfortunately it wasn't to be. When my family got to the police station, they had a copy of his birth certificate and apparently Mama had also managed to secure a copy of the letter

     A Journey from Nowhere to Nowhere

that was sent to me by the social worker to take to school when Ande had to come to live with us in Cape Town. It turned out that there was a copy of that letter somewhere in the house.

The detective who was investigating the case asked some questions of Mom because he wanted to know what her relationship was to the deceased. Yes, the file that he brought with him had Ande's name but really it could be any Ande and not our Ande. He took the copy of the birth certificate and the letter from the social workers and made copies for himself and later told them that he was taking them to Elsiesrivier, where the body was being kept, to see if it was the person they were looking for. Yes, the body had been found in Dunoon on the sports field and the people who were there had told the police that his name was Ande.

He was later identified at a morgue in Elsiesriver and yes, it was him. They were told that the family had three days to remove him from the morgue once he was positively identified. This meant that everything was on track as there was an undertaker on standby already to collect him as soon as it was confirmed. It was now just a matter of the timing: there are stipulated time frames to do things. You can't just rock up and collect your person any time, but the undertakers know that and they know what to do. My mother said it was visible on his face that he had been beaten up using stones or heavy objects, but they never saw the alleged stab wounds.

Lonwabo is said to have looked away when the body was revealed to them. He said he would never traumatise himself by looking at a dead person, injured *nogal*. He wouldn't deprive himself of sleep because of seeing a smiling corpse. I laughed at that one because I never knew that Lonwabo was that bad in terms of being a coward. I mean, I am a coward, but really I have seen a few dead people, especially family.

Ande was collected from the morgue the same day and my family travelled with his body and the undertaker to Nyanga, where they had to sign some documents before his body could be taken home the following day.

Litha had organised men in the village to help dig the grave and had notified the close relatives about his body's arrival at home. Unfortunately, none of us could attend, either from the Mother City or Mahikeng. The most important thing was that he would make it home and he would be laid to rest next to his sister – an end to a terrible journey, a life that never had peace. A painful path of not knowing why your own mother never wanted to see you grow up and become a man. A life of self-inflicted pain to counter the pain that life itself had brought about.

Ande's remains arrived home after a long journey, the very last of his journeys. A journey that he took with no anxiety of what awaited for him on the other side – where he didn't need to worry about what people would say to him. A journey that didn't require him to answer any questions nor speak any word. A journey full of silence… and peace.

Friends, relatives, family and neighbours who could make it were there waiting for him, to bid farewell to him and to pray for his soul. Ande was buried, finally.

◦◦◦◦◦ **Chapter 18** ◦◦◦◦◦

I DON'T KNOW HOW I FEEL about it. I just allowed myself to shelve it as well, exactly the way I did with Zona, but from time to time I can't help thinking about them – how they came about in the first place. How they blended with us. How they lived their lives while growing up among us. The kind of dreams they had. How far they would have gone in life had things not gone the way they did, and mostly how they died. How both of them came into our lives and how they both disappeared on us – one by one.

I sometimes wondered if maybe there was a different way things could have been done and if they would still be alive then. Because I am Christian and I believe in God, I have read Psalms 139 many times and tried to get comfort about this situation, but it has not answered all the questions that I have about this ordeal. Now, as a grown person, having been dealt with by life as well, I have developed ways of protecting myself from any potential hurt; I refused to break down and cry because of the pain that was brought about by this.

From time to time I would find an excuse to justify my feelings, almost as if I were not supposed to be hurt by all of this. The truth is I did get hurt, but I had built this wall around my heart. Then a friend, a therapist, suggested I allow myself to grieve, to mourn, to face my troubles head on and that this would allow me to release all the ill feelings harboured in my heart and would also kick start a whole new process of healing. Because, when I spoke about the things that troubled my heart, the story about my two late siblings always made the list, she pointed out how passionate I became when talking about their issues and how it affected me and how important it was that I deal with it as soon as possible.

As I searched my heart to allow this process, there were a lot of issues that had to be confronted and I realised that theirs was really one of them, if not the greatest. Only then, a year after my younger brother was buried, did I feel that I was ready and would be able to face the reality of their deaths. Yes, I was ready!

I started writing everything down, from the beginning, as far back as I could remember. After a while I made a call to my brother Litha back home. The evening I spoke to him, I sent a voice note to him: "*Broer*, I know that it is almost over eight years now but I need to talk to you about Zona. I want to know, what killed her?"

I think he might have been surprised, if not shocked, by my questions that came from nowhere. I could see that he had listened to the messages but it took him time to respond. The phone would indicate that he was typing out a message and then again he would leave it.

"Awu, Zowi! What makes you to think about that now? It's really been a long time..." he asked, via voice note also.

"I'll tell you why. I can't help it, but I have never dealt with the issue of her death. I didn't understand and somehow I have no knowledge of what caused her to die. I don't remember hearing what caused her to die and now with this guy also dying the way he did, it has not assisted in anyway. Instead, I keep going back and forth. I don't remember anything, even about her funeral," I explained to him.

"Yhoo, sisi! I'm sorry about that but you have to learn to let go…
what's done is done! Their issue is very painful, even to me when I
think about it. It doesn't make sense, but what can one do?" he said.

"Yeah! I guess nothing," I said. "I have managed to dodge it for all
these years and now I have decided to write about it. I hope that this
way I will be able to process it and hopefully to heal."

"Yes, sisi, it is important that you heal so that you can allow them
to rest as well, especially Mamgo. Anyway, Mamgo was killed by
what the doctors called a right flank abscess. They had drained the
abscess from her right flank earlier that day, on the day she passed
on. It would seem that there was also an issue of blood poisoning
and you will know that once something touches your blood stream
then there's no other way but death and in cases like this sometimes
it does not help to question things that have no answers; one just has
to accept. Please, sisi, you have to release them now. Let them rest,
my sister. What happened, happened, sisi. There's no use punishing
yourself." He offered those words of consolation to me.

"Okay, *broer*, I hear you. I'm going to talk to *Mama* and ask if
anyone knew for sure who killed my brother because even there I
never questioned anything, since there were a lot of people saying
different stories… just to find out what she saw when she went to
identify him and what the police said about the cause of his death,"
I said.

"It's okay, sisi, but she did mention that he was beaten up in mob
justice and it was evident by the way he looked when he was identified,
but nobody was arrested for his killing. Like I said, sometimes it does
not help to question things that have no answers; one just has to try
and accept." Litha emphasised what he said earlier.

"Yha nhe! I guess so. And you know what, *broer*? I know by now
that all of us will die eventually and at different times and I know
that life is a journey. We are all on a journey and that journey is

characterised by a lot of things from the day we are born. It's okay, brother, and thank for your time. Also, I apologise for bringing this issue up and please take care…." All this conversation happened via WhatsApp voice notes.

I then had to gather the strength and courage as to how I was going to bring up the topic with my mother. Like I said, it's really not easy to know how people are feeling in my family. I think we all don't know how to express our feelings. You'll be thinking for the person but you don't know for sure because we don't really show emotions. I personally think this is bad. It has not helped me in any way except landing me in a hospital bed on a number of occasions. It was important that I speak to my mother. I thought she'd probably wonder why, a year later, but at the same time she'd understand. She knows me very well. I process things a little later than normal… so I took time out to sit down and have a conversation with Mama.

"Mama! You know, I have been wondering if at some point it became clear as to what or who killed Ande?" I enquired.

"Ey! my child, no. It turned out that he was beaten up by the people in Dunoon. In fact, it's believed that he grabbed something from a person going to work that morning and he was caught and beaten up by the people. No one came forward with concrete information and no one was arrested for that. Even recently, a detective who was handling that case called me to ask if I ever heard any leads," my mother explained.

"*Haybo*! He was asking you that? How come? Are they not the ones who should bring that information to us nah? Mfxm!" I exclaimed in shock.

"No, apparently not. He said there have been no new developments on the case, so he wanted to know if maybe we heard something new beside what was said"

          A Journey from Nowhere to Nowhere

"Okay, I hear this thing of a mob justice but there were stories of him being stabbed *mos* as well?"

"Yeah, there were, but I couldn't see any stab wounds when we went to identify him. He was just badly injured in the face and it was clear that he had been beaten up using different weapons, maybe big stones or something," Mama explained.

"Eish! Mama, this issue of these kids has not settled well within me. It's just sitting somewhere in my mind and it keeps flaring up from time to time and it's confusing and hard to understand the whole thing about their lives, starting from that Zwelibanzi guy..." I elaborated further.

"I understand how you feel, my child. The mystery of these children keeps puzzling me also. How can people just show up, just from the blue, and live like fire made out of straw; burnt out so fast. I mean, just like that!" she said and clapped her hands together.

It was during that conversation with my mother that I learned the truth of how this Zwelibanzi character came to our home and ended up bringing his sister Thembisa who brought her friend Jackie, who eventually abandoned her children at my home.

The Zwelibanzi character came to my family as a young boy of about twelve years old. He was brought to my home by a woman who saw him arriving at her house this one afternoon. He was dirty and had swollen feet. He was hungry, tired and almost looked like he had not seen food for a number of days. As you know, in the village people usually sit in the shade when it is hot, whether under a tree or in shade coming from the shadow of the house. As he approached her house, he is said to have asked for water, food, a place to rest and a job, if possible. This house was one of the few houses if not the only one standing alone very close to the tar road back then.

When asked of his identity and where he came from, as he seemed too young to be looking for a job, he said he was from Reni and that he was a Rhadebe. He told her that he had been taken by some farmer from Umtata, where he had been looking for a job about a week ago. The farmer had picked him up from there to give him a job at one of his farms between Maclear and Ugie.

When he mentioned Rhadebe as his clan name, the woman took him to my home. He then told my parents the same story that he told her, adding that the farmer later dropped him at the farm and left him there alone. He got very scared when he realised that he was the only person left there in that area and thought that something really bad would happen to him. He said he was scared that a giant or some wild beast would come and find him all alone there and eat him up and no one would ever know.

"Any twelve year old would have been afraid, I guess. This boy was too young to be looking for a job or working in the first place," I interjected as Mom narrated the story of Zwelibanzi.

Apparently he said that he had an older sister, Thembisa, and they were both born in Gauteng where they grew up, living with their mother who was a daughter to the MaRhadebe clan from Reni. He said that their mother had died a few years back and their maternal grandfather then took them back home to Reni.

Now, the reason why he ran away from Reni to look for a job was that his grandfather had also passed on and life was really difficult as they were subjected to abuse by his uncles. He said that his older sister ran away first, leaving him behind, and that she had gone back to Gauteng.

As I have said before, my home was always full of people, some who were not even related sometimes. My parents love relatives and it was even worse in this case; it was a child and he was one of us as he was a now considered a nephew, as he was born to a daughter of my clan. Nephews are very special where I come from, by the way – any African will know that. I know how my uncle was to me. So,

 A Journey from Nowhere to Nowhere

my mother prepared water for him to wash and they gave him food, clothes to wear and a place to stay. He stayed at my home and when asked about plans of going home, he made it clear that he didn't want to go there but wanted a job.

After a year or two, while my father was busy with his building work in a village called Mbonisweni, the people where he was building told him they wanted someone to look after their cows and sheep. That was how Zwelibanzi got his second job and left my home to stay in Mbonisweni village and work as a shepherd.

"I hope he wasn't going to be afraid in the middle of it all and leave the flock in the hands of jackals," I chuckled to myself.

"Oh! No, he stayed there, *kanti*." My mom laughed out loud. "He was just a stupid boy in the first instance. Plus, you can imagine a boy who grew up in the township in Gauteng. What did he know about working in a farm?" she said jokingly.

"You can say that again, Mom," I said.

"But he stayed in Mbonisweni and worked and would come home when he had his days off. We laughed about this boy and his ambitions of coming from a township – never been in a village – straight to getting a job in a farm."

Five years after the arrival of Zwelibanzi, my mother was busy with her own things at home when a young lady appeared. She said she was looking for the MaRhadebe family, and that she had been directed to my home.

"And you are?" enquired my mother, looking at this young woman. "Who directed you here? And what do you want?" *I've never seen this girl anywhere before…* were the thoughts that went through my mother's head and she questioned this young lady.

"My name is Thembisa. I am looking for the family where my brother Zwelibanzi stays. He told me that I would find him in this village and when I asked the people that I met at the bus stop they directed me here,"she explained.

"Oh! Okay. You have arrived at the right place, my girl. This is the correct place but your brother is not here. He stays in Mbonisweni, where he works."

This was it! She had reconnected with her brother and he had invited her to come and see the home and the people who had taken him in. Zwelibanzi came back from work for a weekend and told my parents that he had invited his sister to come and see where he was. My father had a goat slaughtered and she was received with warm arms and warm hearts, just as they had received her brother. She is said to have stayed for a few days before leaving for Gauteng again, where she worked. They never saw her again until the fateful day that she returned with Jackie.

Zwelibanzi worked as a shepherd in that village till he was old enough to go and find a job at the mines in Gauteng. He left and was never seen or heard from ever again. Ever!

"This revelation has not given me much as I was hoping to find answers and get closure, but it is still a puzzle that misses a lot of pieces. It's just that I can't help feeling like their journey in life was characterised by abandonment, pain, sorrow, loneliness, betrayal, sickness and drugs and, as painful as what I'm saying is, to me it seems as if it was a journey from nowhere to nowhere, where my family was just a passageway. I mean, these guys came out of nowhere and when I search for them they are nowhere..."

"Yeah! It is a very sad story indeed, sisi, but we need to heal now. It's time to move on now," my mother reckoned.

ꝏꝏꝏ **The End** ꝏꝏꝏ

THIS BOOK IS DEDICATED TO the most important people who have departed this life and hopefully, by the grace of God the Almighty, their souls are resting in peace.

TO MY LATE GRANDMOTHER!

Gambu, Msuthu, Nontuli, Memela, Ngwekazi… I do not for a second doubt your teachings for I am because of them. You did all that a loving and principled parent does for their children. You taught us, and introduced us to God from an early age. Respect for self and for others was the foundation of everything that one could potentially build and kindness was the source of all joy. I guess one must wake up and accept that there was no different way things could have been done in this case. You did your best and it is evident through who I have become. It's just that maybe both Zona and Ande's journey was just a journey from nowhere and going nowhere and all of us were somehow part of a passageway through it, in one way or the other. Even though it is difficult to comprehend their mystery, I remain proud of you and who I have become because of your teachings. May your beautiful soul rest in eternal peace. ♥♥♥

TO MY FALLEN SIBLINGS!

Zonke and Anele… we never chose you, and you never chose us. I believe we were brought together by the grace of God.

You became part of our family and we, yours. Now, family doesn't always mean blood… to me, family is where I'm loved and cherished; where I find warmth and love; where I get guidance and counsel when I go amiss; where both my failures and successes are shared. In many cases I've seen, we grow to have families all over. I don't think we were looking for blood siblings in you; we were aware that it was not possible. We appreciated the bond that came to exist more than blood.

You showed up in our lives and became a huge part of them – and then you disappeared. Life may have not been fair to both of you, but it was not fair to us either – to my family as a whole. Maybe you had a rough start but I believed you would have a better ending… I guess it was not to be. I don't want to know why it all happened because I am not your Creator. He knows best. He fashioned your days on this earth.

I wrote this book remembering you guys, the ups and downs that you went through in this life, together with us, searching for answers and trying to make sense of everything surrounding your life. Also, I know that in the middle of it all you felt like you lost your identities; you felt naked and exposed to what you didn't know. I can imagine that even in death you were confused as to who you were. Having said that, I strongly believe that one's identity is found in God, the Creator, first. You guys knew God and how I wish that in all confusion you had sought Him – maybe you would have found your identities. But secondly I will identify you as *AmaSango amahle, ooNzitha, ooNyandeni'emnyama engathwala ngabafazi, ooPhantsolo, ooKhwayikhwayi kwedini!* Why? Because to me that is who you are to this day. That is who you were and you will forever be until I know otherwise.

I was angry at both of you for different reasons, you know, but this book is part of my conversation that I had with myself after your departure. I've realised that maybe I was not angry but very disappointed. I'm sure you know that I talk too much, so I had to put it down to get it off my chest and now I dedicate it to you guys. My family loved you dearly and how, in my wishful thinking, I wish you had known and believed that. Somehow, it feels as if things would have worked out differently for everyone involved; you and us.

We don't have anything left of you but memories in our hearts and your graves in our garden – and yes, we are scarred for life. Until today, we do not know the woman who left you with us or her whereabouts, but we do know one thing for sure: that we loved you. I pray that the Almighty grants you perfect peace. At least, if you couldn't have that in this life, then in your afterlife may your souls rest in eternal peace and till we meet again. ❤❤❤